Miracles: A Very Short Introduction

VERY SHORT INTRODUCTIONS are for anyone wanting a stimulating and accessible way into a new subject. They are written by experts, and have been translated into more than 45 different languages.

The series began in 1995, and now covers a wide variety of topics in every discipline. The VSI library now contains over 500 volumes—a Very Short Introduction to everything from Psychology and Philosophy of Science to American History and Relativity—and continues to grow in every subject area.

Very Short Introductions available now:

Available soon:

For more information visit our website

www.oup.com/vsi/

Yujin Nagasawa

MIRACLES

A Very Short Introduction

OXFORD
UNIVERSITY PRESS

OXFORD
UNIVERSITY PRESS

Great Clarendon Street, Oxford, OX2 6DP,
United Kingdom

Oxford University Press is a department of the University of Oxford.
It furthers the University's objective of excellence in research, scholarship,
and education by publishing worldwide. Oxford is a registered trade mark of
Oxford University Press in the UK and in certain other countries

First edition published in 2017

Impression: 1

Published in the United States of America by Oxford University Press
198 Madison Avenue, New York, NY 10016, United States of America

British Library Cataloguing in Publication Data

Data available

Library of Congress Control Number: 2017944439

ISBN 978–0–19–874721–5

Printed in Great Britain by
Ashford Colour Press Ltd, Gosport, Hampshire

Contents

Preface

On the face of it, there seems no longer to be a place for miracles in modern society. The renowned German theologian Rudolf Bultmann once remarked, 'It is impossible to use electric light and the wireless and to avail ourselves of modern medical and surgical discoveries, and at the same time to believe in the New Testament world of spirits and miracles.' This remark was made in 1941. One might think that it is even more unreasonable, or perhaps even absurd, to take miracles seriously in the 21st century given our significantly more advanced scientific knowledge and technology.

Yet, surprisingly enough, belief in miracles *is* still very widespread. According to a 2013 Harris Poll, among the 2,250 adults in the USA who responded, 72 per cent believe in miracles. This poll suggests that belief in miracles is only marginally less common than belief in God (74%), and that it is more common than all other supernatural or paranormal beliefs that are listed: heaven (68%), Jesus is God or the Son of God (68%), angels (68%), the resurrection of Jesus (65%), survival of the soul after death (64%), hell (58%), the Devil (58%), the Virgin Mary (57%), ghosts (42%), creationism (36%), UFOs (36%), astrology (29%), witches (26%), and reincarnation (24%).

The UK is considered to be more secular than the USA but belief in miracles is nevertheless widespread. According to a poll conducted by ComRes, CTVC, and Theos in 2013, among the 2,036 adults in the UK who responded, 77 per cent agree with the statement that 'there are things in life that we simply cannot explain through science or any other means.' It is notable that while members of religious groups are more likely to agree with this statement (87%) the majority of non-religious people agree with it as well (61%). Regarding miracles specifically, 30 per cent of respondents think that 'miracles don't exist—they are simply examples of coincidence or luck.' Yet the majority (59%) think that miracles do occur. Moreover, 16 per cent say that either they or someone they know have experienced what they would call a miracle. This poll also suggests that belief in miracles is more widespread than all other supernatural beliefs that are listed: God as a personal being (13%), God as a universal life force (30%), spirits (30%), angels (25%), a higher spiritual being that cannot be called God (12%), the existence of a soul (39%), life after death (32%), heaven (26%), reincarnation (16%), hell (13%), and the power of deceased ancestors (13%).

Given how widespread belief in miracles remains it seems too hasty to declare their demise. In this book, we will address many questions concerning miracles in philosophy, religion, and science. First, what exactly is a miracle? The polls I have mentioned list questions about miracles but neither of them provides a precise definition of a miracle. Hence, it might well be the case that respondents from diverse backgrounds or with widely varied experiences would not agree on what constitutes a miracle. How to define a miracle has indeed been a matter of dispute among philosophers and theologians for centuries. By surveying a number of remarkable examples of unusual events which people may or may not consider to be miracles we will try to reach a satisfactory definition of a miracle.

Second, what miracles are reported in religious texts? There is a close link between religion and miracles. It has been believed for centuries in many religious traditions that such beings as God, angels, and saints can perform miracles. Sometimes miracles are presented as evidence for their religious authority or used as 'tools' to persuade non-believers. We will review miracle reports from the world's great religions and classify them into several types. We will then consider what religious implications we can derive from them.

Third, why do so many people believe in miracles? Again, on the one hand, there seems to be no place for miracles in modern society. Yet, on the other hand, so many people still believe in them. We will address this paradox. The most straightforward solution is to say that miracles really do occur. However, recent research in psychology suggests an alternative answer. According to this answer, belief in miracles is widespread because people are cognitively and developmentally biased towards forming and transmitting such a belief. We will explore relevant scientific findings.

Fourth, is it rational to believe in miracles? This is another question that philosophers have long disputed. Critics argue that we can never rationally believe in them because there can never be evidence strong enough to support the existence of the supernatural. That is, according to these critics, it is always more likely that something that merely *appears* to be a miracle has taken place than that a miracle has really taken place. We will evaluate this argument.

Finally, what can we do if critics are right in saying that we can never rationally believe in miracles? Perhaps we can rationally believe in acts that are comparable to miracles but do not require supernatural intervention. Paradoxically, such acts might be deemed to be just as 'miraculous' as, or even more so than, *real* miracles.

Acknowledgements

I am indebted to Nader Alsamaani, William Barnett, Dan O'Brien, Paul Rezkalla, Sharada Sugirtharajah, and anonymous reviewers for offering helpful feedback, and Joshua Brown for indexing this book. I am also grateful to Martha Cunneen, Andrea Keegan, Jenny Nugee, and Deborah Protheroe at the Oxford University Press for impeccable editorial support. Finally, I would like to thank my family and friends for their love and encouragement.

List of illustrations

Chapter 1
What are miracles?

'Miracles' in sports

The concept of a miracle is an elusive one. We all know roughly
what it is and we can easily cite some well-known examples.
Yet we struggle to state a precise definition. In fact, the proper
definition of a miracle has been a matter of dispute among
philosophers for centuries. An effective way to devise a satisfactory
definition of any intractable concept is to consider a wide range of
concrete examples that represent or misrepresent it. We can then
examine what important features are present or missing in the
examples to make a complete list of necessary and sufficient
conditions that must obtain for the concept to apply. Let us then
start with an example in sports, as many athletes' performances
have been described as miracles:

> At the 1996 Atlanta Olympics the US women's gymnastics
> team hoped to win the gold medal. To accomplish that goal,
> team member Kerri Strug had to earn a score of 9.4 or
> higher on one of her final two vaults. However, on the first
> run she landed badly and sprained her ankle. She scored
> only a 9.1. Seeing her limping, the audience assumed that
> she would have to walk off. However, she did not give up
> and tried the vault one last time. She ran full speed and
> landed perfectly—standing on one foot (Figure 1). She
> scored a 9.7, which brought the team the gold medal.

1. Kerri Strug's performance at the 1996 Atlanta Olympics is often cited as one of the greatest 'miracles' in sports. Strug says that she does not mind that she is always defined by this one moment as she is proud of her performance and she feels fortunate to have had such a moment, which few people have experienced.

The word 'miracle' comes from the Latin *miraculum*, which denotes an object of wonder and amazement. It makes sense that Strug's performance is described as a miracle because it does evoke feelings of wonder and amazement. These feelings arose and continue to arise in witnesses to the event because her performance exceeds their expectations. Yet it seems out of place to call this event a miracle in a strict sense, because it is counterintuitive to think that one can perform a real miracle merely through training and practice. Conversely, if one can perform a miracle through training and practice it is not clear what the distinction is between a miracle and a merely impressive human performance.

'Miracles' in technology

In the same way that a great upset in sports does not seem to count as a miracle, so also a great upset in technology cannot count as a miracle:

> For a long time many scientists were sceptical about the possibility that a manned flight could safely travel faster than sound. Some even speculated that a pilot of a supersonic flight would be torn to shreds. On 14 October 1947, however, Charles E. 'Chuck' Yeager of the US Air Force broke the sound barrier. The speed of his rocket-powered aircraft reached Mach 1.06 without any problem, proving that a manned flight can indeed safely travel faster than sound.

Some describe this event as a miracle because, like the earlier sports example, it represents a marvellous achievement that exceeds people's expectations. Until Yeager's flight in 1947 people had assumed that it was impossible for humans to travel faster than sound. His achievement astonished people by disproving this long-held assumption. Yet it is not exactly a miracle because a miracle should not be achievable simply through an improvement of technology. A miracle should be beyond human control.

'Miracles' in nature

Consider now the following example which represents an amazing event beyond human control:

> About 13.8 billion years ago the universe existed in a state of infinitesimal density and temperature called a *singularity*. The entire universe itself was extremely hot and compressed into an area smaller than that of a pinhead. The big bang then took place, which resulted in the expansion of matter into the vast and cooler universe with many stars. It is estimated that the observable universe has more than 100 billion galaxies and that there are more than 100 billion stars in our galaxy. This means that, assuming there are roughly the same number of stars in each galaxy, there are more than 1 septillion stars (i.e. 1 followed by twenty-four 0s). Note that this includes only stars in the *observable* universe, and so it is smaller than the entire universe, and, moreover, this is based on conservative estimates of the number of galaxies and of the stars in them. There could well be significantly more stars in the universe.

The big bang, which caused the vast size and magnitude of the universe, certainly evokes wonder and amazement in us. It is the biggest and most significant cosmic event ever to have been known to have occurred. The big bang is distinct from the first two examples because it is beyond human control. There is no way that humans could have brought about the big bang. Humans are only minute outcomes of that vast cosmic event. Before the advent of the big bang theory many scientists assumed that there was no beginning of the universe. The discovery of evidence for the big bang was, therefore, a surprise for them. Yet a mere discrepancy between an expectation and an outcome is not sufficient to qualify an event, even an event that is beyond human control, as a miracle. There has to be a deeper link between an expectation and an outcome.

Coincidences as miracles

Consider the following example which involves an astounding coincidence—unusual coincidences are often cited as examples of miracles:

> In 1975, Erskine Lawrence Ebbin was hit and killed by a taxi in Hamilton, Bermuda. It was the same taxi, driven by the same driver, with the same passenger who had also killed Erskine's brother Neville a year before. Moreover, both brothers had been riding the same moped and they had both been 17 years old when they were killed.

Like all other examples that we have seen so far, this example evokes surprise by contradicting our expectations. It seems probabilistically very unlikely that this event could have occurred. Moreover, like the big bang, this unusual coincidence was beyond human control. Furthermore, and most importantly, there appears to be something profound underlying the discrepancy between what one would expect and the true outcome of the event. The big bang example is based on a mere discrepancy between an earlier scientific assumption and the new discovery. On the other hand, in this case, whether or not it is rational, we cannot help but think that there was some deeper, mysterious link between the accident that killed Erskine and the accident that killed his brother Neville a year earlier. Those who are involved in similar tragedies would find it particularly difficult to accept that it was mere coincidence. This element of mystery seems to be an essential ingredient of a miracle. However, it does not seem appropriate to call this twin death a miracle, mainly because it is a tragedy. Indeed, it seems inappropriate for an unwanted event such as this to be called a miracle. Miracles, it seems, cannot have predominantly negative outcomes. Consider, then, another example of a coincidence:

> In 1914, a German mother took a photo of her young son and brought the film plate to a shop in Strasbourg.

She could not collect the photo because the war broke out and she had to leave the city. Two years later she took a photo of her new baby daughter and brought it to a shop in Frankfurt. When she collected the photo from the shop she realized that it showed a double exposure—the photo of her daughter was exposed on a photo of another child. When she looked at it closely she was astonished because the photo of her daughter had been superimposed on the photo of her son that she had taken two years earlier and been unable to collect. For some reason the original film plate that she had used in Strasbourg had been mistakenly marked as unused and subsequently sold in Frankfurt as a new plate. This mother had then purchased the very same plate without knowing that she had used it two years earlier.

This example satisfies all the important features of the previous examples that we have examined. It evokes wonder and amazement, and exceeds human expectations and control. There also seems to be something mysterious and profound underlying the gap between what we would expect and what actually happened. Furthermore, and most importantly, unlike the case of the two brothers, it does not involve tragedy. It is an amazing coincidence that seems completely harmless. Nevertheless, it cannot be appropriately called a miracle because being free from tragedy is still not sufficient to qualify the event as a miracle. A miracle has to have a positive outcome. That is, a miracle has to have a consequence that is wondrous and amazing in a positive, not merely non-negative or neutral, way. Consider, then, the following example of a coincidence:

When Anthony Hopkins landed a role in the 1974 film *The Girl from Petrovka* he decided to read the George Feifer novel on which the film is based. He went to several bookstores in London but none of them had a copy of the book. He gave up and decided to go home. However, while waiting for a train at Leicester Square he spotted a copy of the very book that he was looking for—it was simply lying on a bench. Checking first whether it had indeed been discarded, he picked it up and took it home. Two years later Hopkins met the author Feifer on the set of the film in Vienna. Feifer mentioned to Hopkins that even though he had written the novel he did not have a copy of the book because he had lent his last copy to a friend, who had lost it somewhere in London. Hopkins showed Feifer the copy that he had picked up from the bench in Leicester Square. To their joint astonishment, Feifer confirmed, by looking at handwritten annotations in it, that this was the very copy that he had lent to his friend.

This example satisfies all the required features that we have seen so far. Moreover, it has a positive outcome: Hopkins had been able to find a copy of the book that he needed and Feifer had then retrieved the copy that he had lost. Coincidences with positive outcomes are commonly described as good luck while coincidences with bad outcomes are commonly described as bad luck. Miracles are certainly more comparable to good luck than bad luck. However, even a coincidence with a positive outcome like this one is not exactly a miracle because it is not clear what the alleged mysterious mechanism underlying it could be. One might suggest at this point that a miracle has to involve not merely a vaguely mysterious element but also something that is explicitly religious or supernatural.

Religious signs as miracles

Consider the following example which involves an element that is explicitly religious or supernatural:

In 1994, Diana Duyser of Florida made a toasted cheese sandwich. When she took a bite out of it she saw a face looking up at her. She spotted a burn pattern on the sandwich that looked like the Virgin Mary (Figure 2).

2. The Virgin Mary sandwich had more than 1.6 million hits on eBay. The sandwich was framed and protected by a security guard in a ceremonial cheque exchange. It was sent on a world tour before being sold to benefit a charity.

She was initially scared but then decided to keep it in a plastic box. Ten years passed but the sandwich remained intact. She believed that the sandwich had a special power because during the time that she had it in her possession she won $70,000 at a casino. Eventually, she decided to sell it on eBay (the auction website). She set a starting price of $3,000 with a note of caution saying that it was 'not intended for consumption'. In the end an Internet casino company bought the sandwich for $28,000. Richard Rowe, the CEO of the company, said that he bought it to then raise money for charity.

This example includes most of the required features of a miracle explored so far, such as being wondrous, beyond human control, and exceeding expectations. Given that the sandwich was eventually used to raise money for charity, it can be considered to have had a positive, rather than a negative or neutral, outcome.

Moreover, unlike other examples, this one does involve an explicitly religious or supernatural element. Needless to say, the Virgin Mary is an important religious figure and that is why the sandwich attracted so much attention. Duyser believed that the sandwich had supernatural power that enabled her to win at the casino. Nevertheless, we can hardly consider the cheese sandwich to represent an authentic miracle as it could merely have been a coincidence with religious and supernatural twists. The fact that Duyser sold it on eBay seems to imply that she did not think that the sandwich was genuinely a holy object. The newspapers that reported the event all treated it as a somewhat comical story rather than a serious news item. This observation suggests that a true miracle has to be religiously *significant*; the mere involvement of religious or supernatural elements is not sufficient to make an event a miracle. This leads us to our next example:

A small child riding his toy car strayed onto a railway near his house. The child got stuck on the rail at a crossing because a wheel of his car was trapped by a rail. Unfortunately, an express train was approaching. Because of the curve in the track it would have been impossible for the driver to stop the train even if he had applied the brakes at the moment he saw the child. The mother came out of the house and found her child stuck on the crossing and heard the train fast approaching. She waved and screamed but the child was looking down and did not notice. It seemed unavoidable that the child would be hit by the train. However, unexpectedly the driver *did* apply the brakes early enough and the train stopped within a few feet of the child. An investigation of the event then revealed that the reason the train had stopped without hitting the child had had nothing to do with the presence of the child. The driver had fainted while driving the train and the brakes had been applied automatically as his hand ceased to exert pressure on the control lever. He had been unwell that day due to very high blood pressure caused by an unusually heavy lunch and a fierce argument with a colleague before he had boarded the train. The mother thanked God for saving her son's life.

Unlike the other examples we have seen so far, this one is fictional. It was suggested by the philosopher R. F. Holland as a coincidence that could be considered a miracle. There is a real-life example that is comparable:

At 7:27 p.m. on 1 March 1950, there was a natural gas explosion at the West Side Baptist Church in Beatrice, Nebraska (Figure 3). The timing seemed particularly unfortunate because fifteen members of the church choir regularly gathered there around that time. However, surprisingly, not one of the members was present on that day. Even more surprising was that each of them had somehow had an unrelated and trivial reason not to be there at that particular time. One member and her sister were late because their car had broken down and her friend was running late to pick them up; another was late because he had been taking care of his sons and lost track of the time; another member was late because she had needed to write an important letter; another member and her daughter were late because they had needed to stop at her mother's house before going to the church; and so on. According to one of the members, apart from the day of the explosion no one had ever been late to these meetings. The explosion was so big that it could be heard all around the town—the members of the choir thanked God.

Both of these cases satisfy all the important features of miracles that we have discussed so far and, moreover, they are religiously significant. The mother of the small child believed that God saved her son's life from being hit by the train; and the members of the choir believed that God saved their lives from the explosion. Their beliefs do not appear to be totally unreasonable given how

LIFE'S REPORTS

THE WEST SIDE BAPTIST CHURCH

WHY THE CHOIR WAS LATE

by GEORGE H. EDEAL

It happened on the evening of March 1 in the town of Beatrice, Nebraska. In the afternoon the Reverend Walter Klempel had gone to the West Side Baptist

THE REV. KLEMPEL AND FAMILY

Church to get things ready for choir practice. He lit the furnace—most of the singers were in the habit of arriving around 7:15, and it was chilly in the church—and went home to dinner. But at 7:10, when it was time for him to go back to the church with his wife and daughter Marilyn Ruth, it turned out that Marilyn Ruth's dress was soiled. They waited while Mrs. Klempel ironed another and thus were still at home when it happened.

CONTINUED ON NEXT PAGE

LIFE'S REPORTS CONTINUED

LADONA VANDEGRIFT

Ladona Vandegrift, a high school sophomore, was having trouble with a geometry problem. She knew practice began promptly and always came early. But she stayed to finish the problem.

ROYENA ESTES

Royena Estes was ready, but the car would not start. So she and her sister called Ladona Vandegrift, and asked her to pick them up. But Ladona was the girl with the geometry problem, and the Estes sisters had to wait.

SADIE ESTES

Sadie Estes' story was the same as Royena's. All day they had been having trouble with the car; it just refused to start.

MRS. LEONARD SCHUSTER

Mrs. Leonard Schuster would ordinarily have arrived at 7:20 with her small daughter Susan. But on this particular evening Mrs. Schuster had to go to her mother's house to help her get ready for a missionary meeting.

CONTINUED ON PAGE 22

LIFE'S REPORTS CONTINUED

HERBERT KIPF

Herbert Kipf, lathe operator, would have been ahead of time but had put off an important letter. "I can't think why," he said. He lingered over it and was late.

JOYCE BLACK

It was a cold evening. Stenographer Joyce Black, feeling "just plain lazy," stayed in her warm house until the last possible moment. She was almost ready to leave when it happened.

HARVEY AHL

Because his wife was away, Machinist Harvey Ahl was taking care of his two boys. He was going to take them to practice with him, but somehow he got wound up talking. When he looked at his watch, he saw he was already late.

MARILYN PAUL

Marilyn Paul, the pianist, had planned to arrive half an hour early. However she fell asleep after dinner, and when her mother awakened her at 7:15 she had time only to tidy up and start out.

CONTINUED ON NEXT PAGE

LIFE'S REPORTS CONTINUED

MRS. F. E. PAUL

Mrs. F. E. Paul, choir director and mother of the pianist, was late simply because her daughter was. She had tried unsuccessfully to awaken the girl earlier.

LUCILLE JONES, DOROTHY WOOD

High school girls Lucille Jones and Dorothy Wood are neighbors and customarily go to practice together. Lucille was listening to a 7-to-7:30 radio program and broke her habit of promptness because she wanted to hear the end. Dorothy waited for her.

THE CHURCH AFTER EXPLOSION

At 7:25, with a roar heard in almost every corner of Beatrice, the West Side Baptist Church blew up. The walls fell outward, the heavy wooden roof crashed straight down like the weight in a deadfall. But because of such matters as a soiled dress, a catnap, an unfinished letter, a geometry problem and a stalled car, all of the members of the choir were late—something which had never occurred before.

Firemen thought the explosion had been caused by natural gas, which may have leaked into the church from a broken pipe outside and been ignited by the fire in the furnace. The Beatrice choir members had no particular theory about the fire's cause, but each of them began to reflect on the heretofore inconsequential details of his life, wondering at exactly what point it is that one can say, "This is an act of God."

3. The explosion at the West Side Baptist Church was so strong that it demolished the church and shattered windows in surrounding houses. This forced a nearby radio station to go off the air. One of the choir members says that she vividly remembers the wonderful feeling that she had when she learned that no one had been injured.

probabilistically unlikely it is that these coincidences should have taken place. Although these examples are very close to representing miracles in a strict sense they still seem to miss some essential elements. To ascertain what is missing, it is helpful now to consider some well-known examples that, assuming they are authentic, most people would regard as miracles.

Miracles and impossibility

The following is one of the most well-known examples of a miracle described in the New Testament:

> When Jesus was attending a wedding at Cana in Galilee with his mother and disciples he was told that the wine had run out. Jesus asked servants to fill with water six stone jars that were sitting nearby, and to take some of the filled jars to the banquet. To their surprise, the water in the jars had been turned into wine. The master of the banquet did not know where the wine had come from. He called the bridegroom and said, 'People normally serve the best wine first and then bring out the cheaper wine as the guests get drunk. But you have saved the best one until now.' This was the first sign that revealed Jesus's glory and his disciples believed in him.

Here is another example:

> When Jesus was told that his friend Lazarus was ill he said, 'The sickness will not end in death.' For some reason, he did not visit Lazarus immediately, delaying his trip for two days. When Jesus did arrive he was told that Lazarus had already passed away and had been placed in a tomb. Jesus went to the tomb and said, 'Take away the stone.' Lazarus's sister Martha did not think it was a good idea because there was already a bad odour coming from Lazarus's corpse. However, Jesus insisted that the stone be removed. He then shouted, 'Lazarus, come out!' To the onlookers' astonishment, the

dead man came out, dressed in his grave clothes. Many
people who witnessed this event came to believe in Jesus.

These examples do seem to qualify as miracles. They satisfy all
the important features of a miracle that we have seen so far,
including religious significance. The witnesses to these events
recognized Jesus as divine because of the acts that he performed.
But, why do they seem to qualify as miracles while the survival
of the child on the rail and the survival of the choir members
do not? There appear to be two main reasons. The first is that
while the examples of Jesus's miracles clearly involve acts of an
intentional agent the other examples do not. Jesus intentionally
turned water into wine and intentionally resurrected his dead
friend, while it seems only coincidental that the child was not run
over by the train and that the members of the choir were not
present at the explosion. So we see that for an event to qualify as
a miracle, an intentional agent must bring it about. An event that
occurs naturally does not qualify as a miracle. One might claim
here that an intentional agent, such as God, may indeed have
been involved in the survival of the child and the survival of the
choir members even though the involvement had not been visible.
Even so, there is a further reason to think that these examples do
not qualify as miracles. To see this, we need to distinguish
between distinct types of impossibility.

An event is *probabilistically impossible* if it is impossible as a
matter of probability. For instance, it is probabilistically impossible
for one to be hit by a meteorite ten times purely by chance or for
one to win a multimillion dollar lottery ten times in a row purely
by chance. All the examples of coincidences that we have seen are
comparable to these events. It is probabilistically impossible that
two brothers should be hit separately by the same taxi driven by
the same driver travelling with the same passenger; that the
pattern of burns on a sandwich should turn out to look like the
Virgin Mary; that the driver of a train should faint at the perfect
time to avoid an accident; that fifteen people who are normally

punctual should all be running late on the very day that there is an explosion at their usual destination; and so on. Some of these coincidences are more likely to happen than others but they nonetheless represent events that are highly unlikely to happen. Probabilistically impossible events, however, do not qualify as miracles. This is because probabilistically impossible events are in fact probabilistically *possible* as well, unless the probability of their taking place is exactly zero.

Suppose that it is 99.999 per cent unlikely that brothers should be hit separately by the same taxi driven by the same driver with the same passenger. This event is deemed probabilistically impossible because the chance of its taking place is so slim. That is, ordinary people living ordinary lives do not need to worry about the possibility that such a tragedy will happen. However, saying that it is 99.999 per cent unlikely to happen is equivalent to saying that it is 0.001 per cent likely to happen. Any probabilistically impossible event with more than 0 per cent probability can take place purely by chance. An event that can happen purely by chance cannot be considered a miracle because a miracle has to be an event that is beyond coincidence. (It should be noted that some of these examples are not as probabilistically unlikely as they initially appear. For example, given that billions of pieces of toast are made in the world every day it is not terribly surprising that from time to time people find patterns of burns on them which resemble the Virgin Mary. More generally, given that billions of people living in the world engage in innumerably many activities every day it is not surprising that probabilistically impossible events sometimes do take place.) Miracles invoke awe and amazement because they seem to make what is impossible possible. If probabilistic impossibilities cannot constitute miracles we have to consider some other type of impossibility.

An event is *logically impossible* if it is impossible as a matter of logic. For example, it is logically impossible for anyone to draw a square circle or make one plus one equal four. There could be a community in which a triangle is called a 'square circle' and the number one is called 'two'. In such a community someone could draw what they *call* a 'square circle' or make what they *call* 'one' plus what they *call* 'one' equal four. But that is beside the point. What is meant here is that it is impossible for anyone, as a matter of logic, to draw a figure that could be deemed equally a square *and* a circle; or to perform a mathematical operation in which adding one thing to one other thing would obtain four things. Most philosophers agree that no one, not even an omnipotent God, can perform logically impossible tasks because they would not be genuine tasks. For example, the medieval Christian philosopher and theologian Thomas Aquinas writes:

> [God] cannot make one and the same thing to be and not to be; He cannot make contradictories to exist simultaneously. Contradiction, moreover, is implied in contraries and privative opposites: to be white and black is to be white and not white; to be seeing and blind is to be seeing and not seeing. For the same reason, God is unable to make opposites exist in the same subject at the same time and in the same respect.

Such phrases as 'drawing a square circle' and 'making one plus one equal four' appear to describe tasks because they have the same grammatical structures as phrases that describe ordinary tasks, such as 'drawing a circle' and 'making one plus one equal two'. However, they describe only incoherent 'pseudo tasks' which are not even tasks in the first place. Unlike probabilistically impossible events, logically impossible events can never take place; they are, as a matter of logic, impossible. So the probability of a logically impossible event's taking place is exactly 0 per cent.

Assuming that miracles can take place in principle, they cannot be logically impossible events; logical impossibility is too strong a criterion for a miracle. However, on the other hand, miracles cannot be merely probabilistically impossible events because, again, probabilistically impossible events can take place purely by chance (unless the probability is exactly zero). That is, probabilistic impossibility is too weak a criterion for a miracle. What we need then is a type of impossibility that is weaker than logical impossibility but stronger than probabilistic impossibility. What philosophers call *nomological impossibility* seems to meet this requirement perfectly, and indeed the examples of Jesus's miracles represent nomological impossibilities.

An event is *nomologically impossible* if it is impossible given the laws of nature. For example, it is nomologically impossible to bring about a situation in which a human flies without mechanical assistance or light travels faster than 300,000 km per second. Given the laws of biology and aerodynamics a human can never fly without mechanical assistance and given the laws of physics light can never travel faster than 300,000 km per second. However, there is nothing *logically* contradictory about a human flying without mechanical assistance or light travelling faster than 300,000 km per second. In this sense, they are fundamentally distinct from logical impossibilities, such as drawing a square circle or making one plus one equal four. On the other hand, they are not mere probabilistic impossibilities either because they cannot take place solely by chance. In this sense, they are also distinct from probabilistic impossibilities, such as someone's being hit by a meteorite ten times or winning a multimillion dollar lottery ten times in a row. Nomologically impossible events are those that take place when the laws of nature are violated. For example, a human could fly without mechanical assistance and light could travel faster than 300,000 km per second if the laws of biology, aerodynamics, or physics could be violated.

Let us go back to the examples of Jesus's miracles. Jesus's turning water into wine and resurrecting the dead are miracles precisely because they are nomologically impossible events. Given the laws of chemistry there is no way that water alone can turn into wine. Given the laws of biology there is no way that a person who has been dead for days can be resurrected. Yet they are neither probabilistically nor logically impossible. On the one hand, it is not merely a matter of probability that water cannot turn into wine and the dead cannot be resurrected. These events cannot occur by chance. On the other hand, it is not a matter of logic that water cannot turn into wine and the dead cannot be resurrected. There is nothing logically contradictory about water turning into wine and the dead being resurrected. They are impossible only given the laws of nature in this world. We can construe these examples as cases in which Jesus violated the laws of chemistry and biology so that he could turn water into wine and resurrect the dead. What he performed can be deemed miracles because the impossibilities that they involve are perfectly fine-tuned: they are stronger than probabilistic impossibilities but weaker than logical impossibilities.

Common features of a miracle

We have discussed a number of examples and learned that a miracle has to have the following features:

1. It evokes wonder and amazement.
2. It exceeds people's expectations.
3. It is beyond human control.
4. It suggests a deep, mysterious link between expectations and the outcome.
5. Its outcome is positive.
6. It is religiously significant.
7. It is an act of an intentional agent.
8. It is a violation of the laws of nature.

We can simplify this list. First, it seems that condition (1) can be assimilated into condition (2). A miracle is wondrous and amazing precisely because it exceeds people's expectations. Second, it seems that condition (2) can be assimilated into condition (8). A miracle exceeds people's expectations because it violates the laws of nature, which are not normally expected to be violated. Third, it seems that condition (3) can also be assimilated into condition (8). A miracle is beyond human control because it violates the laws of nature by which ordinary humans are constrained. Fourth, condition (4) can be assimilated into conditions (6) and (7). A deep, mysterious link between expectations and an outcome in connection with a miracle can be attributed to its religious significance and the intention of an agent that brings it about. Fifth, condition (5) can be assimilated into condition (6). The outcome of a miracle is positive in the sense that it has a religiously significant effect on people who experience or witness it. Hence, we are left with three conditions: (6), (7), and (8). With these conditions in hand we can establish the following definition of a miracle:

> A miracle is a violation of the laws of nature that is caused by an intentional agent; and it has religious significance.

Jesus's miracles that we have discussed satisfy this definition perfectly. Jesus is an intentional agent who turned water into wine and resurrected the dead by violating the laws of nature. And his acts made a religiously significant impact on people who witnessed them. The other examples that we examined are not miracles because they fail to meet this definition.

This definition is satisfactory for advancing our discussion. Before closing this chapter, however, some remarks are in order. First, contrary to what the definition may appear to imply, a miracle might in principle involve a negative consequence for some. Consider, for instance, the case of the crossing of the Red Sea described in the Old Testament. God parted the Red Sea in response to Moses's request to let the Israelites cross the sea walking on dry ground. When the Egyptian army reached the sea God, again in response to Moses's request, closed the sea, drowning the Egyptians. Obviously, this event had a positive consequence for the Israelites but it had a negative consequence for the Egyptians. If we consider this as an example of a miracle we have to conclude that a miracle is not always *entirely* positive.

Miracles must have positive outcomes but they could also have negative consequences for some. In this sense, some miracles are analogous to upsets in sports in which, inevitably, the winner's 'miracle' is the loser's tragedy.

Second, it is important to consider who or what can be an intentional agent in the definition of a miracle. The definition is comparable to an influential definition of a miracle introduced by the 18th-century Scottish philosopher David Hume:

> A miracle may be accurately defined, [as] *a transgression of a law of nature by a particular volition of the Deity, or by the interposition of some invisible agent.* (emphasis in the original)

Hume's definition is explicit about an agent that causes a miracle: 'the Deity or some invisible agent'. By this, Hume probably means such an agent to be God, an angel, or some other supernatural being. It is however unnecessary to specify the agent in the definition of a miracle in this manner. If a miracle is a violation of the laws of nature, then whoever brings it about must be a supernatural being. Conversely, if it is not brought about by a supernatural being, it cannot violate the laws of nature in the first place. Notice, however, that it is not the case that every act that a supernatural agent performs is a miracle. For example, even if we assume that Jesus is a supernatural agent his acts within the laws of nature, such as drinking water or walking down a street, are not considered miracles. Also, it is not the case that every event that takes place beyond the laws of nature is a miracle. For example, spirits' communication with each other might take place in a domain that is not governed by our laws of nature. Yet the communication itself would not count as a miracle unless it satisfied other criteria for a miracle.

Ultimately, we can define a miracle, or in fact any concept, as we wish. For example, we can define a miracle loosely as representing a surprising event. However, such a loose definition is not useful because it entails that many events not normally considered to be miracles should in fact *be* miracles. On the other hand, we can define a miracle restrictively as a violation of the laws of nature *by Jesus*. However, such a restrictive definition is not useful either because it entails that many events widely considered to be miracles are not indeed miracles. That is why it is important to develop a definition of a miracle that is neither too loose nor too restrictive. We have seen in this chapter that a miracle can be defined as a violation of the laws of nature that is caused by an intentional agent and has religious significance. This definition might not be perfect but it is sufficient to initiate an informed discussion about miracles.

Chapter 2
What miracles are reported in religious texts?

Production of substances

In Chapter 1, we defined a miracle as a violation of the laws of nature that is caused by an intentional agent and has religious significance. Given that religious significance is an essential element of a miracle it is worth exploring examples of miracles in religious texts. There have been a variety of miracle reports over the course of history. Surprisingly enough, however, there has been virtually no attempt in the literature to catalogue or categorize them to appreciate their diversity. In this chapter, we will overview a wide range of miracle reports in religious texts by classifying them into distinct types.

Miracles are classified into three broad types: material miracles, biological miracles, and mental miracles. Material miracles cause primarily material effects. An act of producing substances out of nowhere is a type of material miracle:

> The Buddha performed the Yamaka-pātihāriya or the 'twin miracle', in which he produced flames from the upper part of his body and streams of water from the lower part of his body. He also produced flames from the right side of his body and streams of water from the left side of his body. Moreover, he alternated flames and streams of water. He performed this miracle for a long time, which no one else could duplicate.

Humans can produce one thing from another but they cannot produce anything from nothing; that would require violating the laws of nature.

When we consider material miracles we have to look at what is produced closely. The Buddha's twin miracle is a production of two *opposing* substances, which is construed as representing his Buddhahood. Miraculous production of food and water is also reported in many religious texts. For example, God in the Old Testament is said to have produced the edible substance *manna* out of nowhere to feed the Israelites in the desert. Muhammad is also believed to have filled an empty well with water and produced food out of nowhere for people in need. Water and food represent what is essential for human survival. In Hinduism, the goddess Lakshmi is believed to have showered gooseberries made of gold on the house of a poor Brahmin woman who had given her last remaining piece of fruit to Adi Shankara, one of the most important exponents of Hindu philosophy. This seems to be a symbolic miracle showing the goddess's recognition of the Brahmin woman's praiseworthy act.

In the Judeo-Christian-Islamic tradition, God is believed to have produced out of nowhere not only individual entities but also the entire universe. This act is referred to as *creatio ex nihilo* ('creation out of nothing').

Transformation of substances

Another type of material miracle is an act of transforming substances radically and instantly:

> To save the Israelite slaves from the oppression of Pharaoh, God caused ten plagues in Egypt. One of them was water turning into blood. Following God's command, Moses and Aaron struck the water of the Nile with their staffs in their hands, which transformed the water into blood. The fish in the Nile died and the river smelled so bad that the Egyptians could not drink the water.

Jesus's transformation of water into wine, which we saw in Chapter 1, is also well-known. Notice that the transformation of a substance is not always a miracle. For example, we can easily transform ice cubes into water by holding them in our hands. This is not considered a miracle because it does not violate the laws of nature. God's transformation of water into blood and Jesus's transformation of water into wine, on the other hand, cannot be performed without violating them.

One might think that transforming a substance is not as impressive as producing a substance. For example, the transformation of clay into a statue is not as impressive as would be the production of a statue out of nowhere. However, when it comes to miracles, transformation does seem at least as impressive as production because the outcome of the transformation (e.g. wine) cannot be obtained merely by processing the original substance (e.g. water). We may speculate here that miracles of transforming substances are in fact versions of miracles of producing substances. For example, when Jesus transformed water into wine perhaps he first produced wine out of nowhere and used it to instantly replace the water.

Multiplication of substances

Miracle workers are believed to be able not only to produce and transform substances but also to multiply them instantly. That is, they are believed to be able to change the quantity, rather than the quality, of substances immediately:

Muhammad gave half a measurement of barley to a man who did not have enough food. His family and guests ate the barley for a long time but it did not run out. Being puzzled they measured it to see how much was left. After that the amount of the barley diminished rapidly. Muhammad said to them, 'If you had not put it to the test by measuring it, it would have lasted you a lifetime'.

Miracles of multiplying food and water are widely reported. Such miracles are celebrated and remembered well probably because, again, food and water are essential for human survival. Muhammad's miracle had a practical purpose: to feed the starving man. Yet what is unique about this episode is that the *termination*, rather than the occurrence, of the miracle gave the man a lesson: we should not question our faith. Like miracles of transforming substances, miracles of multiplying substances might also be versions of miracles of producing substances. For example, when Muhammad multiplied barley perhaps he kept producing new barley out of nowhere as the original barley was consumed.

There are many other examples of miracles of multiplying substances. For instance, in the Old Testament, the prophet Elisha is reported to have helped a young widow who was in debt by multiplying oil in a jar, which was the only valuable thing that she had left in her house. In the New Testament, Jesus is reported to have fed 5,000 people with five loaves of bread and two fish. People who ate them were fully satisfied and twelve baskets of leftovers remained. Similarly, Jesus is also reported to have fed 4,000 people with seven loaves of bread and a few small fish. Afterwards seven baskets of leftovers remained.

Controlling weather

Material miracles include miracles of controlling a variety of natural phenomena. Among the most well-known are miracles of controlling weather:

> Jesus and his disciples were crossing the Sea of Galilee in a boat. Jesus was asleep on the boat but a furious windstorm arose and swamped their boat. The disciples shouted in panic, 'Master, Master, we're going to drown!' Jesus got up, rebuked the wind, and said to the waves, 'Quiet! Be still!' The wind calmed completely. Jesus said to the disciples, 'Why are you so afraid? Do you still have no faith?'

Obviously, an act of controlling weather has an immediate practical benefit: weather is changed in accordance with needs. However, it can also serve as an exemplification of the authority of a miracle worker over nature. Even today's most advanced science and technology cannot always accurately predict the weather—let alone control it. Yet weather also has profound implications for human survival. Flooding could wash out a town and drought could deprive people of food. Storms at sea could drown passengers on ships and the lack of rain in a desert could kill travellers. Jesus's act of calming wind and waves as if they were obedient animals demonstrates his enormous power over nature.

Many examples of controlling weather are found in the Old Testament. For instance, in the narrative of Noah's Ark, God caused flooding by sending rain down on the Earth for forty days and forty nights. His plan was to cleanse the Earth, as the wickedness of the human race had become unbearable. God is also said to have saved Joshua by hurling large hailstones at the Amorite army; and to have sent frightening thunder against the Philistines to help the Israelites. In Islam, Muhammad is said to have saved the people of Medina from drought by causing heavy rain. He is also said to have stopped the rain when their houses were being damaged by it.

Controlling the sun and the moon

Miracle workers are believed to be able to control the sun and the moon as well:

Sceptics challenged Muhammad in Mecca and demanded that he perform a miracle. Muhammad then split the moon into two. One half was seen above a mountain and the other half was seen below it. People were astonished to see the mountain between the two halves of the moon.

Humans are influenced not only by the weather but also by the movements of celestial bodies, particularly the sun and the moon. The gravitational forces of the sun and the moon are strong enough to cause tides on the Earth. The sun in particular is also vital for the survival of organisms as it gives heat and energy. Yet these celestial bodies are so far away from the Earth that we can hardly influence them. Miracle workers' control over remote celestial bodies suggests that they have profound power to control objects without physical means. This power is known as *psychokinesis*.

Religious texts report some other examples of miracles of controlling the sun and the moon. Muhammad is said to have caused the sun to rise early and set late to prolong a day. God in the Old Testament is said to have made the sun and the moon stay motionless so that the Israelites could defeat their enemies. He is also said to have made a day longer by moving the sun back ten degrees on the sundial of Ahaz.

Controlling geographical features

Miracle workers are furthermore believed to be able to control geographical features, such as the sea, mountains, and the earth instantly. The following is an example which we saw briefly in Chapter 1:

When Moses and the other Israelites left Egypt, Pharaoh summoned his 600 chariots to chase them. It seemed impossible for the Israelites to escape when they faced the Red Sea ahead of them. But Moses did not give up. Following God's command he raised his staff and stretched out his hand over the sea. God then drove the sea back with a strong east wind to divide the water and make dry ground. In this way, the Israelites could go through the sea with a wall of water on both sides. The Egyptians pursued

4. *The Children of Israel Crossing the Red Sea*. The crossing of the Red Sea is one of the most dramatic miracles described in the Old Testament. Some scientists speculate that this event might have taken place naturally with the help of a strong, persistent wind and an underlying reef.

the Israelites. Moses then stretched out his hand over the sea again. This time the waters flowed back, sweeping the Egyptians into the sea (Figure 4).

Miracles of this type illustrate miracle workers' power over nature but their practical use seems to be more obvious. Humans build roads, bridges, banks, and tunnels in an attempt to avoid or survive the potential disasters imposed on them by geographical features. Yet it remains impossible for them to control these fully. That is why these miracles are so striking.

Other similar miracles include: the Buddha commanding flood waters to split so that he could walk through them on dry ground; on another occasion he is said to have walked through mountains; in the Old Testament, God is reported to have opened the earth allowing Korah and his company to be swallowed by it when he closed it back up; and Muhammad

is believed to have split a tree into two trunks to make way
for him to pass through.

Walking on water, teleportation, bilocation, and levitation

According to religious texts, miracle workers can also avoid such
obstacles imposed on them as liquidity, time, distance, solidity,
and gravity:

> Adi Shankara called Padmapadacharya and other disciples
> who were standing on the opposite bank of the river Ganga.
> Realizing that boats were not available Padmapadacharya
> started walking on the water. Being impressed by the
> devotion of the disciple to the guru the sacred river placed
> lotuses on the water coinciding with every one of
> Padmapadacharya's steps. He came to be known as
> Padmapada ('lotus footed') because of this miracle.

The Buddha and his disciple Sāriputta as well as Muhammad are
also reported to have walked on water. And it is well-known that
Jesus is said to have walked on water in the Sea of Galilee, with
his disciple Peter following for a short period—although Peter
sank when he was afraid of the wind. These miracles are distinct
from miracles of transforming geographical features, such as God
splitting the Red Sea, because the miracle workers seemed to have
walked on water without moving or transforming the waters
themselves. They succeeded in doing this by overcoming the
human inability to walk on liquid.

Other examples of miracles where human limitations have been
overcome include when Jesus suddenly appeared in a locked
house; when Muhammad made a month's journey from Mecca
to Jerusalem in one night; when Mary of Jesus of Ágreda,
a 17th-century Franciscan abbess, appeared in two places
simultaneously; and when St Joseph of Cupertino, a 17th-century

Franciscan friar, raised his body into the air. These are examples of *teleportation* (moving from one location to another quickly, transcending time, distance, or material obstacles); *bilocation* (appearing in two places at the same time); and *levitation* (rising against gravity), respectively.

Transfiguration

Religious texts also report that miracle workers can change their appearances radically and instantly:

> When Jesus went to a high mountain he transfigured himself in front of his company, including Peter, James, and John. His face shone like the sun and his clothes became extremely white—whiter than anyone in the world could bleach them.

We addressed earlier the Buddha's 'twin miracle', in which he produced flames and streams of water from his own body. We looked at it then as representing a miracle of producing substance but we can also view it as a miracle of transfiguring the self. Transfigurations are performed almost always for symbolic purposes rather than practical benefits. For example, Jesus's transfiguration is understood as showing heavenly glory; and the Buddha's twin miracle is understood as signifying his Buddhahood.

Signs and stigmata

Miracles of displaying signs represent another type of material miracles that have predominantly symbolic purposes:

> In 2009, newspapers reported that verses from the Quran appeared and faded every few days on a 9-month-old baby, Ali Yakubov, in Dagestan. People witnessed the Quranic verse 'Be grateful to Allah' appear in a pinkish colour on the right

leg of the baby. The head of the local region of Kizlar remarked, 'The fact that this miracle happened here is a signal to us to take the lead and help our brothers and sisters find peace'. Thousands of pilgrims came to see the baby.

What is unique about this type of miracle is that a message from a deity is received not spiritually but physically, leaving visible traces on a material object.

Miraculous signs on human bodies are most frequently reported in the Catholic Christian tradition. Stigmata, the inexplicable appearance of marks corresponding to the wounds on Jesus's body on the cross, are particularly well-known. St Francis of Assisi, a 13th-century Italian friar, is considered the first person in Christianity to show stigmata. After encountering an angel he found marks on his hands, feet, and body matching Jesus's wounds. Numerous stigmata have been reported up to the present time. There are also signs that appear on material objects other than human bodies, such as religious statues and icons. There have been reports of statues and icons that bleed, weep, sweat, glow, or produce a special fragrance.

Controlling animals and plants

We have seen numerous examples of material miracles, which cause primarily material effects. Biological miracles, as the name suggests, cause primarily biological effects. The distinction between material miracles and biological miracles is not clear cut because biological effects are forms of material effects. However, it is useful to introduce this category because there are many examples of miracles that cause direct effects on biological entities, such as humans, animals, and plants.

Miracle workers are believed to be able to control animals and plants that are otherwise uncontrollable:

The 13th-century Indian saint and yogi Dnyaneshwar encountered a buffalo when he visited Paithan. The animal was worn out and barely moving. Yet its master tried to move it forward by harshly lashing at it. Dnyaneshwar shed tears of pity and pleaded with the master to give the buffalo a rest. Hindu priests who were watching it ridiculed Dnyaneshwar, saying that he cares more about a dumb beast than the teaching of the Veda scriptures. Dnyaneshwar then placed his hand on the forehead of the buffalo. It started reciting a Vedic song and continued doing so for hours.

Dnyaneshwar's act of making a buffalo recite a Vedic song is understood as a symbolic presentation of his belief that all life is a manifestation of Brahman, or the ultimate reality, according to the Vedas. The moral of this story is that the divine is for all life, not only for elites.

There are many other examples of miracles of controlling animals. In the Old Testament, God is said to have made Balaam's donkey speak; and to have shut lions' mouths to save Daniel. God is also said to have made a fish swallow Jonah and keep him in its belly for three days and three nights until God commanded the fish to spew him out. Muhammad is said to have enabled an old ewe to produce milk; and an exhausted camel that was hardly moving to walk faster than other camels. The Buddha is said to have tamed a wild elephant by touching it when it was about to trample a small child. In the Hindu tradition, the Mother Goddess Durga is believed to have ridden on a lion, which she was given as a gift when she killed the demon Mahishasura. Also, many Indian yogis and sages are said to have controlled animals such as elephants, tigers, and lions.

Miracles of controlling plants are less common but a few reports are found in religious texts. According to the New Testament, for example, Jesus cursed a fruitless fig tree and made it wither from the roots. Muhammad is said to have made a date palm tree weep and then console it when he delivered a sermon. He is also said to have moved the positions of trees instantly and to have made a tree branch move towards him simply by calling it.

Extraordinary childbirth

Childbirth is often described as a miracle because it is a dramatic event initiating new life. Yet ordinary birth cannot be considered a miracle in a strict sense because it does not involve any violation of the laws of nature. Birth miracles are events related to childbirth that do violate the laws of nature. Birth miracles can be classified mainly into two further types: (i) cases in which the conception violates the laws of nature; and (ii) cases in which the delivery or actions of the baby or babies immediately after birth violate the laws of nature. The most well-known example of the first type is probably the Virgin Birth of Jesus:

> God sent the angel Gabriel to Mary, a virgin who was engaged to Joseph. The angel explained to her that she would become pregnant through the Holy Spirit without requiring a human father. Mary was initially very upset by this news but the angel explained to her that God was pleased with her and that she would give birth to a son who would save his people from their sins.

The Virgin Birth of Jesus supports the Christian belief that he is not an ordinary human: he is the son of God. Human conception that does not require both a male and a female is considered a miracle because it is genetically impossible. The Virgin Birth is related to the doctrine of the Immaculate Conception, according to which God ensured that the Virgin Mary was free from the taint of original sin from the moment she was conceived. The Immaculate Conception and the Virgin Birth are often conflated but they are distinct miracles.

Reports of miraculous conceptions are not, however, limited to Christianity. For example, Karna, a central character in the Sanskrit epic, *Mahābhārata*, from ancient India, is said to have been born from his virgin mother Kunti through the sun god Surya. Also, the Hindu deity Vishnu is said to have descended into the womb of Devaki, who gave birth to her son Krishna. A miracle that is contrasted with virgin conception is perhaps conception in a very old woman. According to the Old Testament, God enabled Sarah, who was past childbearing age, to give birth to Isaac.

The following is an example of the second type of birth miracle, in which deliveries of babies or actions of babies immediately after birth violate the laws of nature:

> Maya delivered the Buddha from the right side of her body while standing. It is said that when the Buddha was born he immediately walked seven steps north and at each step a lotus flower appeared (Figure 5). He then stopped and uttered: 'I am chief of the world. Eldest am I in the world. Foremost am I in the world. This is the last birth. There is now no more coming to be.'

The conception of the Buddha itself might not have been a miracle but the way he was delivered and his actions immediately after being born are considered miracles. Like the Virgin Birth of Jesus this signifies that the Buddha is not an ordinary human. It is biologically impossible for a baby to be born smoothly from the side of a mother's body or to walk and speak immediately after delivery. The appearance of lotus flowers makes the Buddha's miraculous birth even more colourful.

There are other examples of the second type of birth miracle. For instance, Muhammad is said to have been accompanied by a bright light when he was born. Laozi, the Chinese philosopher who founded Taoism, is said to have been born as a fully

5. The Buddha is believed to have been born on a full moon day in Lumbini in Nepal around 563 BC. When he was born, an astrologer visited his father and told him that the child would become a great king or a holy man. The Buddha's birthday is known as Buddha Purnima, where 'purnima' means full moon in Sanskrit.

grey-bearded man. The 15th-century Indian mystic poet and saint Kabir is said to have been delivered through the palm of his mother's hand.

Healing

Miracle workers are reported to have healed people with illnesses or injuries. Their acts are considered miracles if they involve one or more of the following: (i) the elimination of a medical condition that cannot be cured by ordinary medical treatment; (ii) the elimination of a medical condition more quickly than is possible by ordinary medical treatment; (iii) the elimination or alleviation of pain that cannot be relieved by ordinary medical treatment;

and (iv) the elimination or alleviation of pain more quickly than is possible by ordinary medical treatment. Among all types of miracles, healing is probably the one that is most commonly reported in all religious traditions. There are several types of healing: physiological, emotional, and spiritual. However, miracles of physiological healing, which involve curing physical illnesses or injuries, are the most widely reported.

Miracles of healing play an important role in beatification and canonization in the Catholic Church. Beatification is an act of recognition by the Pope that a deceased person lived a holy life. It is often based on a posthumously performed miracle. Canonization is an act of recognition by the Pope that the deceased person was a saint. Many canonized figures are believed to have performed more than one miracle. Nearly all miracles that are considered in this context today involve healing. The process towards canonization of a deceased person does not normally start until five years after the person's death. However, Pope John Paul II ruled to fast-track Mother Teresa and start the process only two years after her death due to the first of the following miracles; the second miracle acted to confirm her status:

Monica Besra, a Bengal woman who could not afford an expensive medical treatment, claimed that her stomach tumour was cured by praying to Mother Teresa and pressing a medallion bearing her image on her body. This was recognized as Mother Teresa's posthumous miracle of healing and she was beatified as 'Blessed Teresa of Calcutta' in 2003. In 2008, another posthumous miracle of healing involving Mother Teresa was reported. A Brazilian man had been placed in an intensive care unit having been diagnosed with several brain tumours. Father Elmiran Ferreira Santos gave a medallion bearing Mother Teresa's image to the patient's wife, who then put it under her sick husband's pillow. She prayed with Father Elmiran to Mother

Teresa. Extraordinarily, the tumours disappeared and the husband was discharged from the hospital after a few days.

On the basis of these miracles Mother Teresa was canonized by Pope Francis in 2016, only nineteen years after her death.

These examples involving Mother Teresa can be considered *indirect* healing because no one witnessed Mother Teresa herself healing these patients. It is only inferred that Mother Teresa healed them in response to their prayers to her. It is notable that the examples of indirect healing involved 'mediating items' such as medallions, which appear to link Mother Teresa and the patients. Water is also often used as a mediating item. For example, water from a spring in Lourdes, France, is believed to cure patients who drink or bathe in it. The water is thought to intervene between the Virgin Mary and patients. Lourdes is a well-known pilgrimage site where apparitions of the Virgin Mary were witnessed in 1858. The International Lourdes Medical Committee, comprised of medical doctors, examines reports of miracles at Lourdes. One of the latest miracles authenticated by the committee is the case of Danila Catelli, whose serious health problems were said to have instantly healed after bathing at Lourdes in 1989. This represents the sixty-ninth authenticated miraculous cure at Lourdes.

Unlike indirect healing, direct healing involves a direct interaction between a miracle worker and a patient:

> A woman who had been subject to bleeding for twelve years came up behind Jesus and touched his cloak. Jesus said, 'Your faith has healed you' and her condition disappeared instantly. Jesus walked further and two blind men came to him asking for his mercy. He touched their eyes and their sight was immediately restored. A man who could not speak was then brought in. Jesus drove out the demon possessing the man and restored the man's voice. The crowd praised Jesus saying, 'Nothing like this has ever been seen in Israel'.

Driving out a demon to heal a patient can be construed not only as an example of miraculous healing but also as exorcism, which we will address later. Arguably, miracles of healing are more important than many other miracles because they most clearly exemplify the miracle workers' love and compassion for humanity.

Miracles of healing, including both direct and indirect cases, are reported abundantly in the texts of the world's great religions. For example, in the Old Testament, God is said to have healed the infertility of women and leprosy, restored a withered hand, and prolonged a terminally ill person's life. In the New Testament, Jesus is said to have healed paralysis, dropsy, a withered hand, and deafness. Muhammad is also said to have healed sick eyes, wounds, burnt skin, broken legs, and muteness, and alleviated pain in sick people. In the Eastern traditions, there are a number of health deities. For example, in Manhayana Buddhism, Bhaisajyaguru is known as the Buddha of healing and medicine. In Hinduism there are the Asvins, twin gods of medicine and healing; Dhanvantari, the physician of the gods; Dhatri, a solar god of health and happiness; and Mariamman and Shitala, goddesses of medicine. These deities are believed to have healed many people who have prayed to them and sought their blessing.

Raising the dead and eternal youth

Another form of biological miracle that is comparable to healing is a miracle of raising the dead:

> A child became ill. His condition grew worse and worse as time passed and he finally died. Elijah laid the child on his bed and cried out to God, 'Lord my God, let this boy's life return to him!' The boy came back to life and Elijah gave the boy back to the mother. She thanked Elijah saying that he was a man of God and that the word of God from his mouth was the truth.

Some might view the raising of the dead as an extreme form of healing because both involve restoration of bodily functions. Healing can be understood as the process of recovering an impaired bodily function while raising the dead can be understood as the process of recovering a terminated vital bodily function.

In addition to the examples of raising the dead involving Elijah, the Old Testament reports cases of a dead child who was raised by Elisha; and a dead man who was raised when his body touched Elisha's bones in the same tomb. The New Testament reports some cases of Jesus's raising dead people, including Jairus's daughter, a son of a widow in Nain; and Jesus's friend Lazarus. Jesus himself is also reported to have been resurrected by God, which constitutes a central tenet of Christianity.

Another form of miracle that is comparable to the resurrection of the dead is eternal youth or immortality. It is believed, for example, that Shiva, one of the three main Hindu deities, blessed Markandeya, an ancient Hindu sage, with eternal life and told him that he would forever remain a 16-year-old boy.

Clairvoyance

Thus far we have addressed a variety of material miracles, which cause primarily material effects; and biological miracles, which cause primarily biological effects. Miracles of the third type, mental miracles, cause primarily mental or spiritual effects. These miracles can be classified into three further types: (i) supernatural perception; (ii) control of immaterial beings, such as angels, ghosts, and spirits; and (iii) spiritual communication.

Supernatural perception transcends the five senses (sight, hearing, touch, smell, and taste). In Hinduism and Buddhism, these miracles are associated with the 'third eye', a source of spiritual insight. Clairvoyance is a form of supernatural perception that enables a person to see ongoing events beyond distance or material obstacles without making any ordinary observation, guess, or inference:

> When the Arameans were at war with the Israelites the king of Aram set up camps in various places. However, Elisha supernaturally saw where they were and warned the king of Israel. The king of Aram assumed that someone in his camp was leaking information to the king of Israel. One of the officers told the king, however, that Elisha, the prophet of Israel, could know everything, even words that the king spoke quietly in his bedroom.

The Old Testament also reports that God opened the eyes of Elisha's servant so that he could supernaturally see the enemies' horses and chariots of fire on distant hills. To take another example, Komokuten, a Hindu deity incorporated into Japanese Buddhism, is believed to have had the power to see everything in the world, which is seen represented in his large, gazing eyes.

Retrocognition and precognition

Retrocognition and *precognition* are also forms of supernatural perception. Retrocognition is accurate perception of events that have taken place in the past; and precognition is accurate perception of events that will take place in the future. Like clairvoyance neither of them involves ordinary observation, guessing, or inference:

> When Jesus visited Sychar, a town in Samaria, he encountered a local woman who had come to draw water. Jesus knew supernaturally that she did not have a husband. He told her that he also knew she had had five husbands and that the man she was with at that time was not her husband. The woman was impressed by his supernatural perception and said to Jesus, 'I can see that you are a prophet'.

In this example, Jesus seems to have used both retrocognition and clairvoyance because he knew the woman's past and current situation. The following is an example of precognition from Islam:

> According to Hudhayfah ibn al-Yaman, Muhammad once gave a speech in which he predicted everything that would happen before the Final Hour. Hudhayfah confirmed that Muhammad's predictions had all been coming true.

The importance of clairvoyance, retrocognition, and precognition can be understood in two ways. First, they can be understood as representing, like many other types of miracles, the miracle worker's authority over nature. They show that the perceptions of miracle workers can transcend space and time. Second, they can be understood as representing the enormous epistemic capacity of miracle workers. They show that miracle workers know much more about the world than ordinary humans do.

More examples of precognition than of retrocognition are found in religious texts. This is probably because it is normally more difficult to know accurately what will happen in the future than to know what has already happened. In the Old Testament, it is mentioned that God can tell the future before anything takes place. It reports that God accurately predicted that King Nebuchadnezzar would experience difficult times ahead but also, later, honour and splendour. One of the best-known examples of precognition in the New Testament is an episode in which Jesus told his disciple Peter that, before the rooster crowed, he would deny that he knew Jesus three times.

Mind reading

The last form of supernatural perception that we address here is mind reading, the accurate perception of the mental states of others:

Maudgalyayana was one of the Buddha's chief disciples and was known for his impressive supernatural powers. One day when a group of monks were gathered the Buddha said that the assembly was impure because it included a corrupt monk. Maudgalyayana used his mental powers to scan every monk's mind and located the monk with the corrupt mind. Maudgalyayana asked the monk to leave the room and closed the door. Having confirmed that the assembly had become pure the Buddha began delivering a sermon.

Mental states, such as thoughts and feelings, are understood to be private. That is, there is no direct way to know fully what others think and feel. Miracles of mind reading break such a barrier.

In the Old Testament, God is said to have surveyed the thoughts of many people on the Earth and recognized that they had come to have evil thoughts. Also, David is reported to have told King Solomon that God 'searches all hearts, and understands every intent of the thoughts'. In the New Testament, Jesus is said to have read the minds of people who entertained evil thoughts and also to have opened people's minds so that they could understand the Scriptures. Jesus is also believed to have read the mind of his disciple Judas and predicted his betrayal. (The last example, however, can be considered an example of precognition as well as mind reading.)

Exorcism

We have surveyed mental miracles of the first type, which involve supernatural perception. Mental miracles of the second type involve controlling immaterial, spiritual beings, such as angels, ghosts, and spirits. Miracles of this type include exorcism and apparitions.

Exorcism is a practice to evict demons and other spirits from people, animals, and places:

> When Jesus came to the region of the Gerasenes he encountered a possessed man living in the tombs. The man was so strong that no one could bind him even with an iron chain. Facing the man Jesus said, 'Come out of this man!' A multitude of impure spirits came out and identified themselves collectively as 'Legion'. They begged Jesus not to send them out of the area. Jesus gave permission to them to go into 2,000 pigs feeding on the nearby hillside. The possessed pigs rushed down the steep bank into a lake and were drowned.

Exorcism represents mental miracles because it attempts to evict non-material, spiritual beings primarily with exorcists' mental powers. Exorcism is performed when the possessing spirits are deemed harmful. Exorcism can be construed as a form of healing if it results in recovering the health of a person who was possessed.

Exorcism is practised in nearly all major religious traditions, although many do not see it as a mainstream practice. Jewish exorcism may involve making sacrifices or reciting verses from the Old Testament. Christian exorcism may involve praying, blessing the possessed, or holding a cross (Figure 6). Islamic exorcism may involve reciting verses from the Quran or drinking holy water. Hindu exorcism may involve repeating a mantra or lighting a sacred fire. Buddhist exorcism may involve burning incense, reciting Buddhist scriptures, or making sounds with instruments.

Apparitions

Apparitions are immaterial appearances of supernatural beings or deceased people:

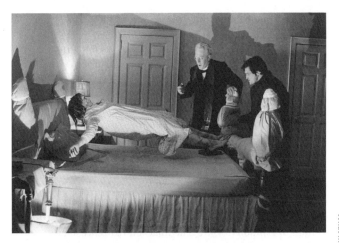

6. The 1973 American film *The Exorcist* popularized the concept of exorcism. In the film, Father Merrin and Father Karras perform an exorcism to save a 12-year-old girl, Regan, who has been possessed by the demon Pazuzu. It was the first horror film ever nominated for an Academy Award for Best Picture.

In the summer of 1916, 9-year-old Lúcia de Jesus Rosa Santos and her cousins saw an angel in a field near the village of Fátima, Portugal. The children were enveloped in strong white light and a cloud formed the figure of a young man who identified himself as the 'Angel of Peace'. They met the angel three times within the same year. On 13 May 1917, they saw a woman 'brighter than the sun' who held a rosary in her hand. She told the children to devote themselves to the Holy Trinity. They understood her to be the Virgin Mary. She appeared every month on the same day, and on each occasion she gave a message to the children. She promised a miracle for her sixth and last apparition, on 13 October. Over 70,000 people, including news reporters, came to witness the miracle. When the rain stopped the sun appeared as a silver disk of changing colours that rotated like a wheel. According to some witnesses, the heat of the dancing sun was so strong that their wet clothes dried instantly. They feared that the miracle might represent the end of the world. The Catholic Church declared that the apparitions at Fátima are worthy of belief.

In her memoir published in 1941, Lúcia claimed that she and her cousins were given three 'secrets' by the apparition in July 1917. The first secret was a vivid vision of Hell, and the second secret was a prophecy about World Wars I and II. In 1960, the Vatican expressed its intention not to disclose the third secret. This led to the hijacking of Aer Lingus Flight 164 flying from Dublin to London in 1981. The hijacker, Laurence James Downey, demanded that the Vatican release the third secret. In 2000, the Vatican finally published the secret, which appears to address the persecution of Christians and the attempted assassination of Pope John Paul II. Some speculate, however, that this represents only a small fragment of the third secret, and that the unpublished part contains more shocking information.

Both exorcism and apparitions presuppose that spirits can exist on their own without accompanying material bodies. That is why they are understood not to be restricted by material obstacles or spatial limitations.

Apparitions are reported in a variety of religious traditions. An angel of God is said to have appeared in flames before Moses from the middle of a bush. The archangel Gabriel is believed to have visited Muhammad when he had his first revelation. The spirits of dead people are said to have appeared to the Buddha's disciple, Maudgalyayana. Some gurus in Hinduism are said to have appeared in places where they could not be.

Spiritual communication

The third and last type of mental miracle that we address here involves spiritual communication, which is also sometimes called *telepathy*:

> Maya and King Suddhodhana did not have children for many years. On a night with a full moon Maya had a vivid dream. In the dream, she was carried away by spirits to Lake Anotatta in the Himalayas. After bathing her in the lake the spirits dressed her in divine robes and decorated her with flowers. A snow-white elephant with six tusks and a white lotus flower came down from heaven, walked around her three times and entered Maya's womb through her right side. She awoke as the elephant disappeared. She took the dream to be an important message because the elephant is a symbol of greatness. She was told later by wise men that she had been chosen to deliver the Purest-One.

Spiritual communication involves direct reception, transmission, or exchange of information between minds without any material means of communication. Miracles of mind reading, which we addressed earlier, can be construed as forms of spiritual communication. This example of spiritual communication preceded the birth miracle of the Buddha, which we also addressed earlier.

It seems that spiritual communication often takes place in dreams. In the New Testament, for example, Joseph is reported to have received a message from God in a dream telling him to flee to Egypt with his family as King Herod was seeking to kill his child, Jesus. Yet dreams are not always necessary. According to the Old Testament, for instance, God appeared to Abraham in a vision to make a covenant promise. In the New Testament, Paul converted to Christianity when he was surrounded by a light from heaven and heard a message from Jesus. These examples of spiritual communication can also be construed as examples of apparitions.

Miracle reports as social, anthropological, or cultural products

We have seen numerous miracle reports found in religious texts from around the world. How should we interpret them? Should we accept them at face value and treat them as testimonies of extremely unusual events? Some maintain that we should not, because miracle reports are mostly social, anthropological, or cultural products.

The British social anthropologist Edmund Leach argues, for example, that the prevalence of specific religious beliefs, including beliefs about miracles, should be seen as reflections of the structure of the society in which they are accepted. Consider the Virgin Birth of Jesus. Leach claims that belief in the Virgin Birth is compatible with a patriarchal social system where rulers are so much superior to the ruled that class difference turns into caste. In such a society the lords never marry people in the lower classes, but they may take concubines from the lower classes. In these cases, the concubines' sons would then be elevated to the ranks of the elite. Leach finds this practice comparable to the Virgin Birth where Mary becomes pregnant through the Holy Spirit and gives birth to Jesus who is the Son of God rather an ordinary human. Leach claims that, throughout history, belief in the Virgin has been particularly strong in patriarchical Christian societies, such as those in the ancient Greek colony Byzantium and in 18th-century Brazil. Leach also notes that Catholic colonialists who believed in the Virgin Birth often pulled their half-caste sons into the ranks of the elite while Protestant colonialists, who tended to reject the Virgin Birth, did not. However, cultural and anthropological explanations such as Leach's must be scrutinized carefully because they often face the chicken-or-egg dilemma: are specific religious beliefs widespread in a certain society because a specific social system is present there? Or is the specific social system present there because the specific religious beliefs are widespread in that society?

Consider another example: some scholars maintain that many well-known miracle reports in religious texts are derived from earlier literary work. According to them, miracle reports should be construed as myths, legends, or fictions rather than as testimonies of extraordinary events. The New Testament scholar Dennis MacDonald, for instance, proposes a controversial hypothesis according to which many episodes in the New Testament run parallel with similar episodes in Greek and Roman epics. He focuses particularly on biblical accounts of Jesus's miracles, such as feeding thousands of people, walking on water, and disappearing into the sky. He argues that parallel miracles are presented in Homer's epic poems the *Iliad* and the *Odyssey*, which are believed to have been written between 750 and 650 BCE. Critics argue, however, that MacDonald's comparison between miracles in Homer's poetry and the New Testament strains credibility.

Even if miracle reports are not social, anthropological, or cultural products it still seems implausible that beliefs in miracles can arise out of nowhere. In Chapter 3, we will consider whether these beliefs can have cognitive or psychological origins.

Why do miracle workers perform miracles?

If we grant that miracle reports are reliable testimonies, the following crucial question arises: why do miracle workers perform these acts in the first place? Performing miracles seems to be extremely risky. Nature is uniform and stable because it is regulated by the laws of nature. If the laws of nature did not exist, we could not breathe, sleep, or even exist. Hence, when miracle workers violate the laws of nature they may endanger living things in nature as well as nature as a whole. There must therefore be specific reasons that they perform miracles despite the risk.

Miracle workers seemingly perform miracles for several reasons. First, they may perform miracles to produce practical benefits for humans, for example when Muhammad multiplied barley to feed a starving man; and God in the Old Testament split the Red Sea to save Moses and other Israelites. Miracles can offer quick solutions to difficulties that humans face. Second, miracle workers may perform miracles to use them as symbolic representations of their teaching, for example when Jesus transfigured himself to show his heavenly glory; and Dnyaneshwar made a buffalo recite a Vedic song to illustrate the universal nature of the Vedas. Miracles can be the most impressive and memorable ways of presenting religious truth. Third, miracle workers may perform miracles to communicate directly with humans, for example when the Virgin Mary appeared to the children in Fátima to give the three secrets; and the archangel Gabriel visited Muhammad to reveal a verse from the Quran. Miracles can be the most efficient ways of communicating with humans. Finally, and perhaps most importantly, miracle workers may perform miracles to demonstrate that, unlike ordinary humans, they have authority over nature and surpass nature. This applies to all miracles because miracles involve, by definition, violations of the laws of nature. Miracle workers prove through these acts that they are supernatural beings who are not constrained by human limitations.

Warnings against dependence on miracles

What do leaders of the world's great religions say about miracles? Interestingly enough, despite the fact that they themselves are reported to have performed miracles many of them are not particularly enthusiastic about miracles. In fact, they often explicitly warn against dependence on miracles.

In Judaism, the Book of Deuteronomy, for example, prohibits occult practices:

> Let no one be found among you who sacrifices their son or daughter in the fire, who practises divination or sorcery, interprets omens, engages in witchcraft, or casts spells, or who is a medium or spiritist or who consults the dead.

The Book of Leviticus makes an even stronger claim: 'Do not turn to mediums or seek out spiritists, for you will be defiled by them'.

Miracles play crucial roles in Christianity. This is manifest in the belief that both the beginning and end of Jesus's life involved miracles: the Virgin Birth and the resurrection. Yet even Jesus advises caution regarding miracles. For example, it is reported that when he was challenged by the Devil he refused to perform the miracles of turning stones into bread or jumping off from the highest point of a temple without getting hurt. Also, when his disciple Thomas did not believe Jesus's resurrection until he actually saw him, Jesus said, 'Because you have seen me, you have believed; blessed are those who have not seen and yet have believed'. Jesus also warned his disciples that when the end of time comes false messiahs and false prophets will appear and they will perform great signs and wonders to deceive people.

Miracles of Muhammad are described in *hadiths*, narrative records of the sayings and actions of Muhammad, as well as the Quran. Yet miracles play relatively small roles in Islam. This is probably because in Islam the Quran itself, which is believed to be a revelation from Allah, is commonly considered to be the greatest miracle. The Islamic scholar Annemarie Schimmel writes that many Muslims would acknowledge that '[t]he performance of miracles is a sign that a person's intention is still directed toward worldly approval, not exclusively toward God'.

The Buddha is also known to have discouraged people from performing miracles. According to one episode, when the Buddha met a yogi who had been trying for years to learn to cross a river by walking on water, he told the man that his effort was a waste of time as he could simply cross the river on a ferry for a small charge. The Buddha presumably thought that a wish to perform miracles would prevent people from being liberated from worldly desires. The Buddha is also said to have condemned Pindola Bharadvaja, one of the Sixteen *Arhats* (saints), who was good at performing miracles. Pindola had succeeded in levitating when he was challenged to do so by a sceptic. The Buddha said to him, however, that miracles should not be performed merely to impress others; they should help people become more enlightened.

The leaders of the world's great religions warn against dependence on miracles, even those that they themselves have performed, because they want their followers to focus on acts that are truly important. Violating the laws of nature is certainly impressive but it does not in itself make that act worthwhile. Indeed, there are acts that are religiously significant even without violating the laws of nature. Conversely, there are acts that violate the laws of nature that are religiously insignificant or even harmful. That is probably why religious leaders think that violating the laws of nature should not be foremost in people's minds when they act in light of their teaching.

Chapter 3
Why do so many people believe in miracles?

The miracle bias hypothesis

We saw in the Preface of this book that, according to recent polls, the majority of people in the USA and the UK today believe in miracles. We also saw in Chapter 2 that reports of miracles can always be found, irrespective of time, geographical location, or religious tradition. How could that be possible? The most straightforward answer to this question is that miracles do really take place everywhere, all the time. However, miracles *should not* be so prevalent. Recall our definition of a miracle: it is a violation of the laws of nature that is caused by an intentional agent and has religious significance. If miracles take place everywhere, all the time, then the laws of nature are being violated everywhere, all the time. If this is indeed so, then nature is so unstable that, it would seem, we should not be able to live normal lives. Suppose, for example, that water was frequently being turned into wine or that dead people were frequently being brought back to life. If these events took place regularly then water supply companies and funeral directors would not be able to run their businesses smoothly. However, we almost never hear them complaining about miracles taking place. If miracles do take place then they are extremely rare events. So that brings us back to square one: why is belief in miracles so widespread?

In recent years psychologists have conducted experiments concerning human cognition, and their results seem to suggest a new hypothesis that answers the question. According to this hypothesis, belief in miracles is widespread because humans are cognitively and developmentally biased towards forming and transmitting such a belief. In this chapter, we will address a number of remarkable recent findings in psychology that seem to support the hypothesis.

Infants and violations of the laws of nature

Miracles evoke wonder and amazement by exceeding people's expectations, and they exceed people's expectations by violating the laws of nature. This means that to recognize miracles it seems minimally necessary that one understand the laws of nature and be able to detect when they are violated. This internal judgement system appears to require a highly sophisticated cognitive mechanism. Surprisingly enough, however, the results of recent psychological experiments suggest that such a cognitive mechanism is already in place as early as infancy. In the experiments in question, children are presented with a set of two events: an expected event, which is consistent with ordinary expectations; and an unexpected event, which appears to violate expectations or the laws of nature. Psychologists have discovered that infants are 'surprised' when they witness unexpected events but not when they witness expected events. The following are some examples:

Infants who were two-and-a-half-months old were shown two areas, left and right, on a mini stage, with a toy lion sitting in the left area. Subsequently, identical screens were placed to hide both areas. The infants were then shown two distinct events. First, as an expected event, they were shown that when the screens were removed the lion remained sitting in the left area. Second, as an unexpected event, they were shown that when the screens were removed the lion now sat in the right area, as if it had instantly teleported from the left area to the right area. According to the psychologists who conducted the experiment, the infants looked for a longer time at the unexpected event than at the expected event.

Infants who were two-and-a-half-months old were shown a tall container with a closed top. Once the container was placed upright another object came from above towards the top of the container. The infants were then shown two distinct events. First, as an expected event, they were shown the object in question resting on the closed top. Second, as unexpected event, they were shown that the object had passed into the container through the closed top as if it could pass through a solid object as a ghost would. According to the psychologists who conducted the experiment, children looked for a longer time at the unexpected event than at the expected event.

These experiments were not conducted with miracles specifically in mind but we can think of the teleporting lion as analogous to a miraculous violation of continuity and the object that passes through the lid as analogous to a miraculous violation of solidity. The psychologists maintain that the fact that the infants looked for a longer time at the unexpected events than at the expected events suggests that they were surprised by the unexpected events. Researchers who have conducted similar experiments have also confirmed children's surprise by observing their facial expressions, pupil dilation, cerebral blood flow, and electrical activity in the brain. Their surprise suggests that infants have certain expectations of the world and that they recognize as discrepancies any divergences from those expectations. In this respect their surprised reactions to the unexpected events are essentially the same as an adult's surprised reaction to a miracle. Adults expect, for example, that water will remain water and not suddenly turn into wine; and that dead people will remain dead and not come back to life. When such expectations are contradicted and they cannot think of any other plausible explanation, they are amazed and consider the events to be miracles.

But do infants' surprised responses serve any purpose? One might think that they are mere reflex reactions that infants display when they witness unusual events. One might also think that since violations of the laws of nature rarely happen, an observation of such an event should not have any cognitive significance for infants. According to some psychologists, however, the observation of an unexpected event might play an important role in the development of cognitive and intellectual capacities. Aimee E. Stahl and Lisa Feigenson argue, for example, that a violation of expectations creates a special opportunity for children and promotes their desire to seek more information about the world. According to them, infants acquire new information about objects that violate expectations more effectively than they acquire information about objects that do not. These psychologists have conducted research on 11-month-old infants. The infants were shown toys which, contrary to their expectations, appeared to pass through a wall or hover in the air. It was found that they spent more time exploring toys that violated their expectations than new toys that did not. The infants were even eager to test their 'hypotheses'. For example, they tried to bang the toys that appeared to go through a wall or drop the toys that appeared to hover in the air, presumably to see if the toys would violate their expectations again or if they could understand how the apparent violations occurred. This suggests that the infants' surprised responses were not mere reflex reactions that served no purpose. A surprise triggered curiosity about objects and motivated infants to acquire more information about the objects and their surroundings. When the very same toys behaved in accordance with their expectations infants did not express as much interest in them. Infants' learning behaviour visibly changes when they see objects that violate their expectations.

Minimal counterintuitiveness

We have seen that children are surprised when they witness events that violate their expectations. This element of surprise seems to play a crucial role in explaining why belief in miracles is so widespread and found in virtually all cultural and religious traditions. The anthropologist Pascal Boyer introduces the so-called *minimal counterintuitiveness theory*, which says that concepts that deviate slightly from intuitive expectations—concepts with a small surprise element—can be transmitted more successfully than common concepts that are compatible with expectations. Let us illustrate this point with an example:

In 1918, Eikichi Suzuki in Hokkaido, Japan bought a traditional Japanese doll in a kimono for Okiku, his small daughter. Okiku loved the doll, and she played with it every day and slept with it every night. However, Okiku became ill and passed away the next year. Eikichi was saddened and he placed the doll in his household Buddhist shrine and prayed over it every day. Okiku's family noticed after some time that the doll's hair seemed to have grown. When Eikichi had bought the doll for Okiku, its hair had reached only around the ears but now it clearly reached its shoulders. People thought that Okiku had loved the doll so much that her spirit had possessed it. As time has passed, the hair has grown even further and it has reached the back of the doll. The doll is now placed at the Mannenji temple in Hokkaido. The mystery of the doll is widely known in Japan.

Sceptics speculate that the doll's hair appears to have grown because of the way it was implanted in the 'scalp'. According to them, the actual length of the doll's hair is longer than it initially appeared as the extra length is necessary to plant and tighten the hair. Over time, they say, the tie must have become loosened and the hair must have become stretched. Hence it looks as if the hair has grown. Whether such a speculation is correct is not, however, our concern here. What is of interest is why this kind of story spreads so easily. This story has many variations. The names of the people involved and the years mentioned in the story vary with its retelling. How, when, and who noticed the growth of the doll's hair also vary. Yet, the surprise element of the story, namely, the alleged growth of the doll's hair, is present in all versions. This corresponds to what psychologists call a minimally counterintuitive concept. Dolls' hair is not expected to grow because, of course, they are not alive. The growth of Okiku's doll's hair, therefore, deviates from our intuitive expectations and it is this minimal counterintuitiveness which has most likely led to the story being transmitted so easily, spreading throughout Japan.

Suppose that the story had not involved the growth of the doll's hair and that it had simply been a story about a father who had kept a doll in memory of his daughter. Lacking the surprise (or minimally counterintuitive) element, such a story probably would not have spread as successfully as did the widely known story. Suppose then that the story had involved *more* counterintuitive elements. We can suppose, for example, that not only the doll's hair but also its body had grown. Moreover, we could add that the colour of its kimono had constantly changed and that the eyes of the doll had shone at night. If surprise elements contribute to the transmission of a story, then one might assume that the more surprise elements we add the more widely and persistently a story will transmit. According to the minimal counterintuitiveness theory, however, that is not the case. For a story to transmit successfully it has to involve the right amount of counterintuitiveness. The number of surprise elements involved cannot be too few but also not too many. The psychologist Justine Barrett says that minimally counterintuitive concepts are perfect for being remembered and transmitted because, on the one hand, they avoid over-taxing people's conceptual systems by being relatively straightforward but, on the other hand, they offer an idea that is challenging enough to attract additional attention.

Barrett and Melanie Nyhof have conducted a number of experiments that support the minimal counterintuitiveness theory.

For example: fifty-four American students were asked to read science fiction stories about an inter-galactic ambassador visiting a museum. The stories were designed to include an appropriate number and type of concepts. The inter-galactic ambassador in the stories sees the following three types of exhibits in the museum:

1. Counterintuitive items such as a living thing that never dies. Each of these items has a feature that violates intuitive assumptions about the object.

2. Bizarre items, such as a living thing that weighs 5,000 kilograms. Each of these items has a highly unusual feature but does not violate intuitive assumptions about the object.

3. Common items, such as a living thing that requires nutrients to survive. Each of these items has a feature that is intuitively expected.

In order to determine how stories are transmitted through people, the experiment involved three 'generations' of students. The students in the first generation read one of the science fiction stories twice. After two minutes they were instructed to type out the story as best they could from memory. Students in the second generation were instructed to read two retellings of the story written by students in the first generation. They were then asked to retell the two retellings that they had read as one story. This procedure was repeated for the third generation. The psychologists found that participants recalled counterintuitive items better than bizarre items, and bizarre items better than common items. They also found that after three generations of retelling some items had shifted: some items that had begun as bizarre became common; some items that had begun as common became bizarre; and so on. But by far the largest type of shift was from bizarre to counterintuitive.

Boyer and Charles Ramble conducted comparable experiments in France, Gabon, and Nepal and confirmed that the minimal counterintuitiveness theory applied across cultures. This seems to hint at why miracle stories are common irrespective of geographical location or religious tradition.

The studies that we have seen were conducted in controlled experimental settings. Does the minimal counterintuitiveness theory apply to the real world? To answer this question, Anders Lisdorf studied ancient Roman prodigies, short episodes of unusual events that were circulated and reported to Roman officials from 218 to 44 BCE. The ancient Romans had a sophisticated system for processing prodigies. Some of the best-known rumours were reported to a magistrate, who in turn reported them to the senate, which decided whether the signs in the reported events should be accepted. If they were accepted, they were interpreted by the senate itself or the major priestly colleges. Each prodigy therefore went through several levels of transmission in oral and written form, not unlike what happens with modern urban myths. The prodigies involved counterintuitive concepts (such as milk rain, sudden openings in the ground, and a statue of a Roman goddess crying); bizarre concepts (such as a praetor and a consul dying in office unexpectedly, an unusual sighting of an owl in the city, and rare occurrences of food meant for a goddess being eaten by a dog); and common concepts (such as storms, flooding, and the burning of a palm tree). Lisdorf confirmed that among 605 prodigies, the majority (56%) involved counterintuitive concepts, while 41 per cent involved bizarre concepts, and only 4 per cent involved common concepts. Among the counterintuitive concepts, 99 per cent involved one violation of expectations, 1 per cent involved two violations, and none involved more than two violations. This seems to support the minimal counterintuitiveness theory.

Throughout history, there are many well-known miracle reports containing good examples of minimally counterintuitive concepts. Jesus's turning water into wine or resurrecting the dead involves surprise elements that are based on violations of the laws of nature yet do not deviate from expectations in an overly complex manner. It seems that these miracle stories have survived for centuries because they strike a good balance by being counterintuitive enough to attract people's attention but not so counterintuitive as to confuse them.

Detecting agents' faces and voices

Again, on our definition, a miracle is a violation of the laws of nature that is caused by an intentional agent and has religious significance. Setting aside religious significance, the definition involves two key components: (i) a violation of the laws of nature; and (ii) an intentional agent. What we have seen is relevant to the first component. Interestingly enough, psychologists have also conducted research which is relevant to the second component. Their findings seem to suggest that people have a cognitive or developmental bias towards detecting agents in nature.

The anthropologist Stewart Guthrie argues that religion arises from a human tendency to attribute characteristics of agents to natural objects and events. While this tendency creates many false beliefs it is, or for a long time it was, beneficial to survival. If humans see the shadow of an object in the woods, for example, it is better for their survival to recognize it as a predator. Guthrie maintains that we constantly scan our environment and look for agency because of the survival advantage. If a suspicious object turns out to be something harmless, then that is not a big loss—better safe than sorry. Guthrie tries to account for the prevalence of religious beliefs by appealing to such a cognitive tendency. Barrett calls the hypothetical cognitive system responsible for detecting agents the 'hyperactive agency detection device' (HADD). Empirical studies suggest that all people have the HADD and that it is already active in the first five months of life.

In Chapter 2, we addressed episodes involving a burn pattern on a toasted cheese sandwich that looked like the Virgin Mary. The recognition of such a pattern represents so-called *pareidolia*, a psychological phenomenon of misperceiving a pattern in a vague or obscure stimulus. This phenomenon is closely related to the HADD. Patterns on pieces of toast are randomly produced traces but people 'find' meaning in them as if they were paintings. Pareidolia does not have to involve an image on a flat surface. For example, Rebekah Speights in Nebraska found a Chicken McNugget that looked like George Washington. After keeping it for three years, in 2012 she sold it for $8,100 on eBay. To take another example, the JCPenney department store placed a stainless steel tea kettle promotion on their billboard advertisements in 2013. It was not the intention of the maker but people found the kettle to resemble Adolf Hitler extending his right arm. The kettle was sold out soon after the resemblance was reported worldwide through social media.

Examples of pareidolia can be on a much larger scale. For example, the 'Old Man of the Mountain', a cliff face in the White Mountains of New Hampshire in the USA, was widely known because of its resemblance to a human face. A natural rock formation on Heimaey, an Icelandic island, is known as the 'Elephant Rock' because it looks like a giant elephant dipping its trunk into the sea. A similar example is even found on another planet. The spacecraft Viking 1, while circling Mars to find a possible landing site for another spacecraft, took an image of a geographical structure that looks like an Egyptian Pharaoh. Some speculated that this structure, which is now known as the 'Face on Mars' (Figure 7), was created by Martians. However, images that were taken by other spacecraft later confirmed that the structure is a flat hill, which only looks like a face from a certain angle.

Detection of faces is important because faces are among the most distinctive features of agents and it is crucial for survival in nature to detect agents, especially predators. It is then not surprising that

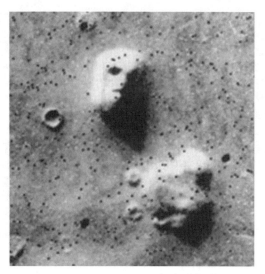

7. The 'Face on Mars' has become a popular icon since the spacecraft Viking took its image in 1976. More recent high resolution images suggest, however, that it is only a hill with a flat top. In some cultures a human face is also recognized in the disc of the full moon.

psychologists find that babies, even newborns, pay more attention to toys that have facial features, such as eyes, nose, and mouth, than to those without.

Detection of faces plays an important role not only for humans but also for many animals, including insects. For example, the larvae of *Eudocima tyrannus*, a moth found in Asia and Russia, have distinctive patterns on their bodies that look like big eyes, making them look almost like cartoon characters (Figure 8). There are also owl butterflies, which have large eyespots on their wings. As their name suggests, the spots make them look like owls. These false eyes serve the purpose of scaring away predators. Some species of pygmy owl also have eyespots on the backs of their heads. They act to confuse predators about the direction in which the owls are facing. Similarly, foureye butterflyfish have

8. Eudocima tyrannus is a moth found in Russia, China, India, Japan, and the Philippines. The insect uses mimicry effectively. The larva has eyespots on the body to deceive predators and the adult has wings that provide camouflage among dried leaves.

black dots that look like eyes on the rear of each side of the body, tricking predators on their expected direction of travel while they swim away in the opposite direction. These examples of mimicry in nature do not represent pareidolia because pareidolia involves misperception of a familiar pattern in a random pattern while these example of mimicry involve misperception of a familiar pattern in a non-random pattern. Nevertheless, the examples of mimicry in nature teach us how crucial detection of agency is for the survival of organisms.

Pareidolia does not have to be present in visual experiences. It can be present in other sensory experiences, such as auditory experiences. In the 1973 film, *The Exorcist*, there is a scene in which a tape of gibberish from a possessed girl is found to contain a message when it is played backwards. This scene popularized the concept of *backmasking*, a recording technique that involves reversing an audio signal that is meant to be played forwards.

Some people then claimed that popular rock songs contained Satanic messages when they were played backwards. For example, in 1982, Led Zeppelin's 'Stairway to Heaven' was alleged to contain reversed hidden Satanic references, such as 'Here's to my sweet Satan' and 'I sing because I live with Satan' during the middle section of the song. Led Zeppelin's record company denied the allegation and issued a statement: 'Our turntables only play in one direction—forwards'. Many examples of songs that are alleged to contain Satanic messages are posted on the Internet with captions to highlight the messages. The captions encourage listeners to hear the Satanic messages that are supposedly there but without the captions these messages are not audible.

There are also examples of pareidolia in parapsychology. Some ghost hunters and parapsychologists advocate 'electronic voice phenomena', where voices of sprits are said to be heard in electronic recordings. The investigation of electronic voice phenomena was motivated by an article by Thomas Edison published in the October 1920 issue of *Scientific American*. In the article he says:

> I have been thinking for some time of a machine or apparatus which could be operated by personalities which have passed on to another existence or sphere ... I do claim that it is possible to construct an apparatus which will be so delicate that if there are personalities in another existence or sphere who wish to get in touch with us in this existence or sphere, this apparatus will at least give them a better opportunity to express themselves than the tilting tables and raps and ouija boards and mediums and the other crude methods now purported to be the only means of communication.

Enthusiasts of electronic voice phenomena place recording devices at relevant locations and analyse what was recorded to see if spirits have left any signs of trying to communicate with them. Often they have to put a lot of effort into finding messages as purported voices of spirits are faint or difficult to hear over other noises. Examples of electronic voice phenomena are posted on the Internet, but like the examples of alleged Satanic messages in rock songs, listeners would not detect any messages without captions. Animals misperceive predators in visual experiences. We can reasonably assume that they misperceive predators in auditory experiences as well. We can speculate, for example, that certain animals are biased to detect the roar of their predators in random noises.

Faces and voices are among the most distinctive signs of the presence of agents. If so, the cognitive bias towards detecting them might explain why belief in miracles—which, according to our definition, must be caused by agents—is so widespread.

Detecting the intentions of agents

According to our definition of a miracle, an agent that causes a miracle has to be an *intentional* agent: that is, a being with free will and the ability to act in accordance with purpose. Faces and voices, however, represent mainly the presence of agency and not necessarily agents' intentions to act in a certain way. Hence, the fact that humans are biased towards detecting faces and voices does not necessarily suggest that humans are also biased towards detecting intentional agents. Recent research in psychology, however, suggests that humans are also biased towards detecting intentions and purposes in nature.

The 20th-century Swiss psychologist Jean Piaget attributes *artificialism* to children—the tendency to think that physical objects in nature, such as planets and mountains, are created by agents. Piaget's theory is contentious but psychologists have recently conducted relevant research that seems to provide indirect support. Deborah Kelemen, who has done extensive research on this topic over the last few years, maintains that even if children are not exactly artificialists as Piaget conceived of the term, they might be considered *intuitive theists*, as they are biased to see things in nature as purposefully designed by God or a similar agent. One of Kelemen's experiments runs as follows:

Forty-eight elementary-school children and sixteen adults were shown four pairs of realistic, hand-drawn pictures of unfamiliar prehistoric animals and unfamiliar non-living natural objects. For instance, one of the pairs consisted of pictures of an aquatic reptile and a pointy rock. They were then given questions about the features of the pictured objects, such as, 'Why do you think aquatic reptiles had such long necks?' and 'Why do you think the rocks were so pointy?' They were given several possible answers and asked to pick ones that made the most sense to them. There were three types of possible answers: (i) explanations of the physical type not appealing to any purpose, such as 'The aquatic reptiles had long necks because the stuff inside got all stretched out and curved' and 'The rocks were pointy because little bits of stuff piled up on top of one another over a long time'; (ii) explanations of the self-serving type appealing to purpose, such as 'The aquatic reptiles had long necks so that they could grab at fish and feed on them' and 'The rocks were pointy so that animals wouldn't sit on them and smash them'; (iii) explanations of the social type appealing to purpose, such as 'The aquatic reptiles had long necks so that they could hold up their friends when they got tired from swimming' and 'The rocks were pointy so that animals like the aquatic reptiles could scratch on them when they got itchy'. Kelemen has found that children tend to prefer explanations of the self-serving or social type that appeal to purpose over explanations of the physical type that do not appeal to any purpose.

It is notable that the results of the experiment suggest that children tend to think that the features of non-living natural objects as well as of living objects exist for a purpose. That is, they tend to believe that objects of all kinds are 'made for' something. This does not mean that children cannot distinguish between natural objects and artefacts. On the contrary, recent empirical studies suggest that children do distinguish them through perceptual information, knowledge about the origins of ordinary human artefacts, and information about natural essence. This also does not mean that children cannot distinguish between intentional and unintentional acts. On the contrary, according to recent empirical studies, even 12-month-old babies understand that, in everyday situations, only intentional agents can create order from disorder. Kelemen conducted an experiment similar to the one that we have seen but on children in the UK this time, where religion is culturally less influential than in the USA. Her results revealed that British children exhibit the same tendency to prefer explanations appealing to purpose.

How did adults respond to the questions about aquatic reptiles and pointy rocks? They were more selective in applying explanations appealing to purpose. For example, they did not apply explanations appealing to purpose to non-living natural kinds such as pointy rocks. Also, while they applied self-serving explanations appealing to purpose to biological features they did not apply social explanations appealing to purpose to them. This seems to suggest that adults are not as strongly biased as children towards detecting intention in nature. One might therefore conclude that these psychological findings are not relevant to miracles because most miracles are witnessed and reported by adults. Such a conclusion seems hasty, however, because another psychological experiment suggests that adults are *implicitly* biased towards explanations appealing to purpose:

One hundred and twenty-one university students were divided into three groups. They were all shown a series of explanations for a wide range of phenomena on an overhead screen and asked if they thought they were good or bad explanations. Students in the first group were asked to respond in a 'normally speeded' condition. Students in the second group were asked to respond in a 'moderately speeded' condition. Students in the third group were asked to respond in an 'extremely speeded' condition. Kelemen and Rosset found that, on average, students in the extremely speeded condition mistakenly chose 47 per cent of the incorrect explanations appealing to purpose such as 'Ferns grow in forests because they provide ground shade' and 'the sun radiates heat because warmth nurtures life'. This is a significantly greater proportion than the proportion of students who chose such incorrect explanations in a moderately speeded condition (36%), which was in turn greater than the proportion of students who chose them in the normally speeded condition (29%).

The results of the experiment suggest that people, even educated adults, have an implicit bias towards believing explanations appealing to purpose. When they have limited processing time they are more likely to choose incorrect explanations appealing to purpose. As people acquire correct scientific knowledge they suppress their innate disposition to appeal to purpose. This disposition does not, however, seem to disappear completely. The existence of an implicit bias towards believing explanations appealing to purpose suggests that not only children but also adults are biased towards seeing intention and purpose in nature. Again, this seems to explain why belief in miracles, as acts of *intentional* agents, is so widespread.

Detecting supernatural beings

The psychological findings that we have discussed suggest that humans are biased towards detecting intentional agents in nature. It is not obvious, however, that the agents have to be specific supernatural beings, such as God or angels. 'Agents with intention and purpose' could refer to ordinary humans or animals. In order to show that people are biased to believe in miracles it has to be shown that they are biased to detect supernatural beings in particular. Piaget makes a claim that bears on this point. He concludes through his interviews with children that many children younger than 7 years old tend to ascribe attributes of God, such as sanctity, omniscience, omnipotence, eternity, and ubiquity, to adults, especially to their parents. As many parents experience, small children often assume that their parents know everything and can do everything; they are surprised or even disappointed when they learn that this is not the case. Piaget quotes such examples as a girl asking her aunt to make it rain and a boy being perplexed to hear his father saying something that was not true.

Piaget's point makes sense because there is a survival advantage for small children in trusting adults unquestioningly. By utterly trusting adults' knowledge and power, small children can acquire new information and skills that are useful for securing food and shelter. Adopting a sceptical stance towards adults, on the other hand, is not beneficial to them in this respect. Barrett even speculates that, just as children over-estimate the knowledge and power of adults, they might over-estimate the morality of adults as well. That is, children might ascribe not only omniscience and omnipotence but also moral perfection to adults. These observations seem to imply, at least indirectly, that humans are cognitively biased towards detecting not only an intentional agent in general but a *supernatural* intentional agent such as God specifically.

The findings in psychology we have considered in this chapter provide cumulative support for the hypothesis that belief in miracles is widespread because humans are cognitively and developmentally biased towards forming and transmitting such a belief. This, however, does not mean that all miracle reports are false or untrustworthy. Consider a parallel example. Suppose that psychologists find that humans have a cognitive bias towards seeing cans of beer in their fridges when they are thirsty—this does not mean that there can never be cans of beer in their fridges. It may very well be the case that there always are cans of beer in their fridges. Similarly, the fact that people are biased towards forming a belief in miracles does not mean that there are, therefore, no miracles. Nevertheless, the psychological findings give us an important lesson: We should always resist taking miracle reports at face value. Perhaps it is possible for miracles to take place but we should evaluate miracle reports very carefully, certainly more carefully than reports of ordinary events. In particular, we should pay attention to possible underlying cognitive and developmental biases in the reports.

Chapter 4
Is it rational to believe in miracles?

The most crucial question concerning miracles

We have addressed many questions concerning miracles—How can we define a miracle? What types of miracles are reported in religious texts? How do psychologists explain the formation and transmission of belief in miracles? However, we have yet to address the most crucial question—Can we rationally believe in miracles? Let us address this question by scrutinizing existing arguments against belief in miracles.

Hume and miracles

Undoubtedly the best-known critic of belief in miracles is David Hume, an 18th-century Scottish philosopher. He is widely recognized as the founder of the modern debate over miracles. His sceptical stance towards supernatural beliefs is illustrated in an episode that occurred at the end of his life.

The author and lawyer James Boswell visited Hume in Edinburgh near his death and recorded the last interview with him. As Boswell describes him, '[Hume] was lean, ghastly, and quite of an earthy appearance.... He was quite different from the plump figure he used to present.... He said he was just approaching to his end.' Boswell asked Hume if he would reject the possibility of an afterlife even when he was facing death before his eyes. Hume's answer was that while it is 'possible that a piece of coal put upon the fire would not burn' it is 'a most unreasonable fancy that we should exist for ever'. Boswell also asked Hume if the thought of annihilation ever gave him any uneasiness. Hume responded, 'not the least; no more than the thought that [I] had not been'. Boswell continued, 'Well, Mr. Hume, I hope to triumph over you when I meet you in a future state; and remember you are not to pretend that you was joking with all this infidelity'. 'No, no', said Hume. 'But I shall have been so long there before you come that it will be nothing new.'

In his book *An Enquiry Concerning Human Understanding*, Hume defines a miracle as 'a transgression of a law of nature by a particular volition of the Deity, or by the interposition of some invisible agent'. This definition is a starting point of any philosophical discussion of miracles. As mentioned in Chapter 1 of this book, it is comparable to our definition: a miracle is a violation of the laws of nature that is caused by an intentional agent and has religious significance. Based on his definition of a miracle, Hume introduces several arguments against miracles. It is important to examine them carefully as they are considered among the most powerful such arguments.

There has never been enough evidence for miracles: Hume's first four arguments

Hume makes two main claims against miracles: (i) as a matter of fact there has never been enough evidence for miracles; and (ii) as a matter of principle it is always unreasonable to believe in miracles. Consider claim (i) first. Hume provides four arguments for this claim and they can be summarized as follows:

Argument 1: For any testimony to give us full assurance that a miracle has occurred, it must satisfy several conditions. For example, there has to be a sufficient number of witnesses with enough good sense and education to enable them to avoid being deluded. These witnesses must also have undoubted integrity thanks to which no one needs to worry that they will be deceitful. They must also have social standing or reputations which would be damaged if their testimony were discovered to be false. They also have to attest to what they have witnessed in such a public manner that any false claims are guaranteed to be revealed. However, no one has ever given testimony of a miracle which satisfies these conditions.

Argument 2: People tend to believe in extraordinary events such as miracles because they have a passion for events that inspire wonder. Even people who do not experience miracles at first hand are delighted to listen to miracle reports and enjoy exciting the admiration of others. This tendency intensifies when the spirit of religion joins the love of wonder. Religious people may imagine things that have no reality and believe what they know to be false for the sake of promoting their religious views. Vanity and self-interest operate on them more powerfully than in any other circumstances. Miracle reports are comparable to news of marriages. There is nothing that arises so easily and spreads so quickly in country places and provincial towns than such news. People take great pleasure in telling and spreading them, and strongly desire being the first reporters. This observation applies equally to miracle reports.

Argument 3: People who believe in miracles live mainly in 'ignorant and barbarous nations'. There are some civilized people who believe in them but they inherited their beliefs from their ignorant and barbarous ancestors. If we look at history, many events were once explained in terms of supernatural concepts such as prodigies, omens, oracles, or judgements, but these explanations have been eliminated as history has progressed towards the enlightened ages. The most ignorant and barbarous of the barbarians carry miracle reports abroad where people lack sufficient information and authority to refute them. Moreover, people's interest in the marvellous makes miracle reports spread very widely.

Argument 4: It is impossible for all religions to be true because they make conflicting claims. A miracle report that seems to establish a particular religious system therefore overthrows another system. For example, any miracle report that purports to establish the authority of Christianity undermines the authority of Islam. Conversely, any miracle report that purports to establish the authority of Islam undermines the authority of Christianity. Similar reasoning is commonly adopted in the courts. For example, a judge may conclude that the credibility of a pair of witnesses who maintain that they saw a crime against a certain person occur is undermined by the testimony of another pair of witnesses who claim to have seen the person in question a few hundred miles away when the crime was committed.

The four arguments from Hume help to remind us how cautious we have to be when we assess miracle reports. However, they seem not to succeed in establishing the conclusion that Hume intends to derive: as a matter of fact there has never been enough evidence for miracles. Let us cast a critical eye on each argument in turn.

Argument 1 lists several conditions which Hume thinks witnesses of miracles have to meet. Yet the conditions are specified only vaguely. It is not clear, for example, how many witnesses are required or what sort of educational backgrounds they must have. Hume, however, gives the impression that a miracle report cannot be considered authentic without a very large number of witnesses who are perhaps comparable to Hume himself in terms of education, reputation, and social status. However, if that is what he really has in mind, then Argument

1 sets the standard too high. Historians and judges, for instance, conclude all the time that certain historical events took place or certain crimes were committed without requiring such a high standard. In response to this point, Hume might lower the standard and contend, for example, that only a dozen or so witnesses with relevant educational qualifications, such as degrees in science, would suffice. However, this new standard is problematic because it is relatively easy to meet. Proponents of miracles would argue that there have indeed been cases of miracles that meet this standard. In summary: Argument 1 is problematic for two reasons. First, it specifies a required standard too vaguely. Second, even if it specifies a required standard clearly it is still problematic. On the one hand, if the standard is set high then we have to give up making judgements regarding ordinary historical events and crimes. On the other hand, if the standard is not set high then Hume would have to admit that certain miracle testimonies meet his standard.

Argument 2 purports to undermine belief in miracles by pointing out that when witnessing apparent miracles people tend to react passionately with surprise or wonder, and feel an urge to spread interesting news. This is an insightful observation because it is compatible with the findings in 21st-century psychology which we addressed in Chapter 3. The word 'miracle' comes from the Latin *miraculum*, denoting an object of wonder and amazement. As the meaning of the word suggests, miracles normally involve elements of surprise, which are based on violations of the laws of nature. As we saw in that chapter, psychologists contend that the elements of surprise typically correspond to what they call minimally counterintuitive concepts, concepts that minimally deviate from our intuitive expectations. Many well-known examples of miracles, such as Jesus turning water into wine or Buddha walking and speaking immediately upon birth, are good examples of minimally counterintuitive concepts. Psychologists maintain that minimally counterintuitive concepts are perfect for being remembered and transmitted because, on the one hand, they avoid over-taxing people's conceptual systems by being relatively straightforward but, on the other hand, they offer an idea that is challenging enough to attract additional attention.

Hume's Argument 2 is consistent with psychologists' account. It is not obvious, however, that the tendency to experience feelings of surprise or wonder or the urge to spread interesting news undermines miracles in the way Hume intends. Suppose that Hume is right in saying that there is nothing that arises so easily and spreads so quickly in rural places and provincial towns than news of marriages. The tendency to be excited about hearing and spreading such news means false rumours are likely to be easily produced and spread. However, of course, it would be a mistake to conclude from this observation that there has never been, for example, enough evidence that people get married. At most, we can conclude that we should be cautious when we hear rumours about marriages. If we apply the same reasoning to miracles, we can conclude nothing more based on Argument 2 than that we should be cautious when we hear reports of miracles. Hence, while Argument 2 makes a good point it does not undermine belief in miracles in general.

Argument 3 seems to be based on Hume's somewhat snobbish way of thinking about belief in miracles: belief in miracles is common mainly among people in 'ignorant and barbarous nations'. Similar thinking seems to underlie Arguments 1 and 2 as well. How does Hume decide which nations are ignorant and barbarous? Hume might answer this question by saying that a nation is ignorant and barbarous if most people there hold irrational beliefs such as belief in miracles. However, such an answer would make Hume's reasoning circular because it entails that Hume is making the trivial claim that miracles are believed in by people who believe in miracles! Perhaps it is more charitable to think that what Hume really has in mind in advancing Argument 3 is that miracles are believed mainly by people in nations where there are not enough educational opportunities. If people have enough education to understand how nature operates, according to this idea, they would not believe in miracles in the first place. However, this interpretation would also make Argument 3 unsuccessful because it does not reflect reality. As we saw in the Preface of this book, statistics show that belief in miracles is widespread even in such nations as the USA and the UK, where people generally enjoy better educational opportunities than in many other nations. It should also be noted that Hume is incorrect in thinking that belief in miracles is destined to be eliminated as history progresses. Again, statistics show that belief in miracles is common even today, centuries after the Age of Enlightenment. Hence, contrary to what Argument 3 says, belief in miracles has been prevalent irrespective of geographical locations and time.

Argument 4 says that miracle reports within distinct religious traditions undermine one another because they make contradictory claims. According to Hume, this is analogous to a situation in which a pair of witnesses claim that a certain person committed a crime while another pair of witnesses claim otherwise. Hume is right in saying that miracle reports can appear to undermine one another in a certain sense. For example, Christians and Muslims can appear to be in conflict if Christians try to prove the truth of Christianity by appealing to reports of Jesus's miracles while Muslims try to prove the truth of Islam by appealing to reports of Muhammad's miracles. The apparent conflict comes from the assumption that Christianity and Islam cannot be true simultaneously. This is, however, irrelevant to whether or not miracles in general can ever occur. Christianity and Islam *do not* conflict with respect to the possibility of miracles in general. On the contrary, reports of both Jesus's miracles and Muhammad's miracles motivate the claim that miracles can occur. This means that Hume's example of people witnessing a crime is not exactly analogous to cases of people witnessing miracles. The following example seems to be more analogous: Suppose there is a dispute about a person's death. Some think this is a case of homicide and others think it is a case of suicide. A pair of witnesses claim that they saw a man in a blue shirt murdering the person. Another pair of witnesses claim that they saw a man in a green shirt murdering the person. Even though the two pairs are making conflicting claims with respect to the *colour of the shirt* of the murderer, they are in agreement with respect to the *cause of the victim's death*. Analogously, even though Christian witnesses of miracles and Muslim witnesses of miracles make conflicting claims with respect to which religion is true they are in agreement with respect to the possible occurrence of miracles. Argument 4, therefore, fails to undermine belief in miracles.

It is always unreasonable to believe in miracles: Hume's main argument

As we have seen, Hume's four arguments for claim (i), that as a matter of fact there has never been enough evidence for miracles, seem unsuccessful. However, he also advances claim (ii), that as a matter of principle it is always unreasonable to believe in miracles. Hume's argument for claim (ii) is regarded as his main argument against miracles and, arguably, it raises a greater challenge for believers in miracles.

To defend the unreasonableness of belief in miracles, Hume appeals to the following principle: the strength of a belief should be in proportion to the evidence for it. Suppose that Hannah is your trustworthy friend. If she says that she saw a fox around her house, it is reasonable for you to assume that she did see a fox around her house. The very fact that *she* says that she saw a fox around her house is strong enough evidence to convince you that she did see a fox around her house. There is nothing extraordinary about her claim as foxes have been seen in her suburb. Also, she has never lied to you and there seems no reason for her to lie to you this time. Moreover, Hannah can easily distinguish foxes from other animals as she is an animal lover. Hence, if you proportion your belief to the evidence, then it is reasonable for you to believe that Hannah did see a fox around her house. Suppose, on the other hand, that Hannah says that she saw a Martian around her house. Even if Hannah has never lied to you, it is unreasonable for you to believe that she did see a Martian around her house, *unless* there is strong evidence to suggest that she really saw a Martian around her house or that she is an extremely reliable source of testimony even when it comes to visitors from other planets. This extra evidence is required because it is significantly less likely that Hannah saw a Martian around her house than that she saw a fox around her house. Hence, if you proportion your belief to the evidence, then, given the lack of extra evidence, it is unreasonable for you to believe that Hannah did see a Martian around her house.

Carl Sagan, a renowned American astronomer and the author of the novel *Contact*, on which Robert Zemeckis's 1997 film of the same name was based, makes a similar point in response to the claim that extraterrestrials are the cause of seemingly unusual events in the Bermuda Triangle:

> There's not a smidgen of evidence to suggest that lights in the sky or the disappearance of ships or planes are due to extraterrestrial intervention. The return of those planes is a favorite incident of the most uncritical panderers of the Bermuda Triangle mysteries. *Extraordinary claims require extraordinary evidence.* (emphasis added)

Sagan's now widely known slogan 'extraordinary claims require extraordinary evidence' is an application of Hume's principle that the strength of a belief should be in proportion to the evidence for it. It is unreasonable for you to believe that extraterrestrials cause lights in the sky, or ships and planes to disappear because it is an extraordinary claim lacking extraordinary evidence. Similarly, it is unreasonable for you to believe that Hannah saw a Martian around her house because it is an extraordinary claim lacking extraordinary evidence.

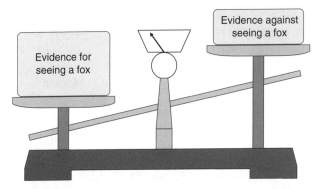

9. The weight corresponding to evidence for Hannah's seeing a fox around her house on the left pan is heavier than the weight corresponding to evidence against it on the right pan. It is therefore rational to believe that Hannah did see a fox around her house.

To illustrate Hume's and Sagan's principles, consider an imaginary balance scale that can weigh evidence for and against the occurrence of any event. Let us now place evidence for Hannah's seeing a fox around her house on the left pan of the scale and evidence against it on the right pan. We can confidently say that there is sufficient evidence for believing that Hannah did see a fox around her house because the balance scale indicates that what is on the left pan is much heavier than what is on the right pan (Figure 9). That is, the evidence for Hannah's seeing a fox around her house is much stronger than the evidence against it. Hence, you have more than sufficient evidence for your belief that Hannah saw a fox around her house; you do not violate Hume's and Sagan's principle if you hold such a belief.

Let us now place evidence for Hannah's seeing a Martian around her house on the left pan and evidence against it on the right pan. We can confidently say that there is sufficient evidence for believing that Hannah did not see a Martian around her house because the balance scale indicates that what is on the right pan is much heavier than what is on the left pan (Figure 10). That is, the evidence for

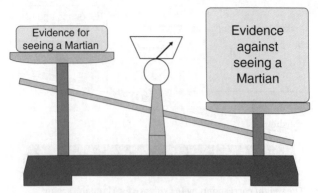

10. The weight corresponding to evidence for Hannah's seeing a Martian around her house on the left pan is significantly lighter than the weight corresponding to evidence against it on the right pan. It is therefore not rational to believe that Hannah saw a Martian around her house.

her seeing a Martian around her house is much weaker than the evidence against it. Hence, you have less than sufficient evidence for the belief that Hannah saw a Martian around her house; you do violate Hume's and Sagan's principle if you hold such a belief.

Let us then place evidence for a miracle taking place on the left pan and evidence against it on the right pan. The crucial question is whether the balance scale indicates that what is on the left pan is heavier than what is on the right pan. Consider a specific example of a miracle: the resurrection of a dead person. Evidence that we could place on the left pan includes a medical confirmation certifying the person's death; testimony from many people witnessing the person's being alive after the confirmation of death; and so on. Hume allows us to place as much evidence as we can find for the resurrection on the left pan. Yet he says that no matter how much evidence we gather it can never be heavier than the evidence against the resurrection on the right pan.

To see Hume's point, recall that both his definition and our definition require that a miracle should violate the laws of nature. This means that evidence against miracles (e.g. resurrections) consists of the laws of nature themselves because the laws of nature, by definition, prohibit miracles. The laws of nature provide extremely strong evidence—possibly the strongest evidence we can imagine—against miracles because they are established on the basis of firm and uniform observations of the operation of nature. This evidence is so strong, Hume says, that no evidence for miracles can be strong enough to contradict it. In other words, no evidence for miracles that we place on the left pan of our balance scale can be as heavy as evidence against miracles on the right pan. Hume maintains that if we are to rationally believe that a miracle has taken place, it has to be the case that it is more extraordinary, or more 'miraculous', to reject the occurrence of the miracle than to accept it. However, he says, it is always more extraordinary to *accept* the occurrence of a miracle than to reject it because accepting it requires us to reject the laws of nature, which are stable and consistent. Hence, according to Hume, in any circumstances, we have less than sufficient evidence for miracles: we do violate Hume's and Sagan's principle if we believe that a miracle has taken place.

Let us illustrate Hume's point with another example. Suppose that 100 great scientists from all over the world witness an act of turning water into wine. They observe the act very closely and record it from many angles with the most advanced technology. They also sample the water and the wine, and analyse them in detail. They also examine the alleged miracle worker thoroughly to exclude any suspicion of fraud. The scientists spend a long time examining the collected data independently to ensure that they have not made any mistakes. They all confidently conclude that the water was indeed turned into wine. Suppose that the only alternative explanation that is remotely plausible is that each of the 100 scientists from all over the world happened to hallucinate when they observed the act of turning water into wine or analysed relevant data over a long period. Needless to say, the coincidence that they should all experience hallucination at the same time is incredibly unlikely to happen. Yet, Hume would say that it is still more reasonable to believe this implausible explanation than the explanation that the miracle really occurred. However unlikely it is, the hallucinations of 100 scientists can in principle occur without violating the laws of nature. Yet, a miraculous transformation of water into wine cannot even in principle occur within the laws of nature. Using the terminology introduced in Chapter 1, we can express this point as follows: 100 scientists hallucinating for an extended period is only probabilistically impossible; however, water turning into wine miraculously is not only probabilistically impossible but also nomologically impossible—impossible even in principle given the laws of nature. Hume generalizes this reasoning and concludes that it is always unreasonable to believe in miracles.

Implications of Hume's argument

Hume's argument is a matter of enduring philosophical dispute. Nevertheless, whether or not the argument ultimately succeeds, the following two points are clear. First, the argument is not necessarily bad news for believers in miracles because, contrary to common perception, it does not completely exclude the possibility that miracles occur. The argument shows, if it is successful, only that it is always unreasonable to believe that miracles take place. The claim that it is always unreasonable to believe that certain events take place does not entail that these events can never take place. For example, perhaps it is always unreasonable to believe that a volcanic eruption occurs on a planet in a remote galaxy because it is impossible to gather enough evidence for it. This does not, however, entail that there can never be a volcanic eruption on that planet. Similarly, it might well be the case that even though we can never accumulate sufficient evidence for miracles, as violations of the laws of nature, miracles actually do occur. Such a possibility is compatible with Hume's argument.

Still, Hume's argument is not necessarily good news for believers in miracles because it shows the enormous difficulty of rationalizing belief in miracles. Thus the second point we can assert is that the argument shows, even if it ultimately fails, that it is incredibly difficult to justify believing that miracles have really taken place. Suppose that Hume's argument is fallacious and that there can be sufficient evidence for a certain miracle. Even so, it would still be extremely difficult for us to gather such evidence because it has to be strong enough to overturn the laws of nature, which appear to be more consistent and uniform than anything else that we know of. We can put this point another way by appealing to the analogy of a balance scale again: the evidence against a miracle on the right pan is so heavy that it would be unimaginably difficult, even if it is in principle possible, to gather heavier evidence on the left pan. Hence, even if Hume's argument ultimately fails, that is, even if it is in principle possible to justify belief in miracles, it might well be the case that gathering enough evidence for miracles is practically impossible. In other words, even if we directly encounter a miracle we would struggle to convince others and even ourselves that a miracle has really taken place.

Chapter 5
Can there be miracles without the supernatural?

Altruistic acts of Kolbe and Williams

The most unique feature of miracles is their violation of the laws of nature. Miracles evoke surprise and amazement precisely because they do not follow the ordinary course of nature. We have seen, however, that it is this very feature that makes it difficult to justify belief in miracles: the laws of nature are not meant to be violated; they are confirmed through solid and uniform scientific observation. If belief in miracles cannot be justified, what are the closest acts to miracles that we can rationally believe in?

Maximilian Kolbe was a Polish Conventual Franciscan friar who was born in 1894. In 1941, his monastery was shut down and he was arrested by the German Gestapo. The reason for the arrest is unclear but some attribute it to his publication criticizing the Nazis. Kolbe was first taken to the Pawiak prison and then to the Auschwitz death camp. One day a prisoner from Kolbe's barracks escaped the camp. To deter further escapes, the deputy camp commander picked ten prisoners to be sent to the starvation bunker. One of the selected prisoners was Franciszek Gajowniczek, a Polish army sergeant who had been separated from his wife and two sons. When he was chosen he cried out, 'My wife! My children!' Listening to his cry, Kolbe volunteered to take his place, declaring, 'I want to go instead of the man who was selected. He has a wife and family. I am alone. I am a Catholic priest.' Kolbe was permitted to go to the bunker instead of Gajowniczek. Bruno Borgowiec, a Polish prisoner who was assigned to service the chosen prisoners, describes the situation in the cell as follows:

The ten condemned to death went through terrible days. From the underground cell in which they were shut up there continually arose the echo of prayers and canticles. As the days went by, the number of survivors lessened. The man in charge of emptying the buckets of urine found them always empty. Thirst drove the prisoners to drink the contents. Father Kolbe never asked for anything and did not complain: he encouraged the others, saying that the fugitive might be found and then they would all be freed.

Those in the cell died one after another but Kolbe and three others were still alive after two weeks. The authorities therefore decided to kill the four by injecting them with carbolic acid. Kolbe gave his arm to the executioner while praying; he died on 14 August 1941 at the age of 47. Gajowniczek, who had been saved by Kolbe, spent more than five years in concentration camps but he survived the war. His two sons had been killed in the war before his release, but he was reunited with his wife, Helena. She died in 1977, but Gajowniczek lived until 1995 and died at the age of 93. When Gajowniczek passed away his second wife Janina remarked that 'he had a deep sense of Kolbe's presence' and that she believed that 'he has gone to Kolbe' (Figure 11).

Shusaku Endo, the Japanese Catholic author who is best-known for the novel *Silence*, on which Martin Scorsese's 2016 film of that name was based, maintains that Kolbe's act counts as a miracle.

I can never perform an act like Kolbe's and I get scared even by the thought of acting like him. It is never possible for ordinary folk like myself to die for someone else. Yet Father Kolbe performed such an act. *This is what I call a miracle because a miracle is an act of love*

11. A West German stamp bearing an image of Maximilian Kolbe commemorates his beatification by Pope Paul VI in 1971. Kolbe was canonized by Pope John Paul II in 1982.

that ordinary people cannot do. He exemplified the verse in the Book of John: 'Greater love has no one than this: to lay down one's life for one's friends'. (emphasis in the original)

Let us call an act such as Kolbe's—sacrificing one's own life to save a stranger's life—an 'extremely altruistic act'. Kolbe's extremely altruistic act does not count as a miracle according to our definition because it does not violate the laws of nature. Endo's claim that it is a miracle, therefore, seems too strong. Yet, the act seems to be comparable to a miracle. Kolbe's act is commonly discussed in a religious context because he was a Catholic priest. However, extremely altruistic acts are also reported in non-religious contexts.

A deep freeze was blasting Washington, DC, on 13 January 1982. Air Florida Flight 90 took off from Washington National Airport but the aircraft failed to gain altitude, and hit cars and trucks on the Rochambeau Bridge, killing four people. It then smashed into the Potomac River, which was covered by thick ice. Among the seventy-nine people on board only six escaped the sinking plane, clinging to the tail of the airplane above water. A rescue helicopter arrived but the situation did not look promising (Figure 12). The river was filled with jagged ice and the survivors were rapidly losing strength. The rescuers had to act quickly. Each time they threw a life ring from the helicopter to the

12. The crash of Air Florida Flight 90 killed seventy-four people on the plane and four motorists on the bridge into which it crashed. The snowstorm and icy water made the rescue operation perilously difficult.

survivors, Arland D. Williams Jr. grabbed it and handed it to another survivor instead of using it for his own survival. The sky was getting dark and the temperature started to drop. Williams continued handing the life ring to others until all of them were safely on shore. However, when the helicopter went back to rescue Williams for the last run, he was not there. He had already sunk into the deep icy water and was tangled in the wreckage.

His identity was not known for a while and the media referred to this mystery hero as the 'man in the water'. It was reported later that he was a 46-year-old bank examiner from Atlanta, a divorced father of two who was engaged to be remarried. A year after the tragic event, the Rochambeau Bridge was renamed the Arland D. Williams Jr. Memorial Bridge to honour his altruistic act.

Again, according to our definition of a miracle, extremely altruistic acts, such as Kolbe's and Williams's, are not miracles because they do not violate the laws of nature. Yet we may treat them as acts that are closer to miracles than any others because they evoke awe and amazement by being so like a violation of the laws of nature. Instead of violating the laws of nature, extremely altruistic acts defy strong behavioural traits entailed by those laws. Nature is governed by the process of natural selection, which involves competition for survival. For approximately four billion years, uncountably many organisms have competed and struggled for survival. Nature is like a cruel game in which organisms constantly fight for limited resources and are rewarded by an increase in their fitness—the ability to produce offspring in a particular environment. The weaker organisms are thus destined to be eliminated. We are alive now because our ancestors were successful in surviving and reproducing in this violent game. The evolutionary biologist Richard Dawkins remarks, 'natural selection is out there and it is a very unpleasant process. Nature is red in tooth and claw.' If we try to kill a spider, for example, it will do its utmost to run away. This is not because it has the concept of danger and is trying to avoid it but because, roughly speaking, it has developed, over many generations, the behavioural trait of avoiding danger thus increasing its fitness. Similarly, humans avoid danger, especially life-threatening danger, because death would reduce their chance of surviving and reproducing to zero.

Miracles evoke awe and surprise partly because they violate the laws of nature. Similarly, extremely altruistic acts evoke awe and surprise because they too violate, through the altruistic person's own will power, a strong behavioural trait that humans have acquired through the long process of evolution. Gajowniczek, who was saved by Kolbe's altruistic act, remarked, 'I was stunned and could hardly grasp what was going on. The immensity of it: I, the condemned, am to live and someone else willingly and voluntarily offers his life for me—a stranger. Is this some dream?' It is beyond belief when someone sacrifices his or her own life to save a stranger because humans are not supposed to act like that in the survival game of nature. Yet extremely altruistic acts are not subject to Hume's argument, which says that it is never reasonable to believe in miracles. It can be perfectly reasonable to believe in extremely altruistic acts because, unlike miracles, they do not violate the laws of nature.

Somewhat paradoxically, extremely altruistic acts could be considered as 'miraculous' as, or possibly even more so than, what we have defined as miracles, *because* they do not violate the laws of nature. If Kolbe had possessed supernatural powers enabling him to violate the laws of nature, perhaps he could have easily produced food to avoid starvation or teleported himself and the other prisoners to a safe location. Similarly, if Williams had possessed supernatural powers perhaps he could have easily prevented the crash of the plane by stopping the snowstorm; or rescued himself and the other victims by emptying the river instantly. However, their extremely altruistic acts evoke awe *because* they did not have these powers. Facing near-certain death, they did not give up hope and instead tried their best to save strangers, exhibiting love, compassion, and charity to the maximum extent. Endo writes:

> I would not think of it as a miracle if bread had suddenly fallen from heaven or lights from heaven had blinded the Nazi officials when the priest was sent to a starvation bunker. What is important is the fact that to save the crying young man in front of him Kolbe said without a sense of despair, 'I don't have a wife or a child as I am a priest. Let me substitute him', and voluntarily went to the starvation bunker only to die. I want to say that this fact *is* a miracle.

Again, Endo's claim that Kolbe's act is a miracle cannot be true given our definition of a miracle. Yet he seems right in thinking that Kolbe's act is comparable to a miracle and that a violation of the laws of nature is not always essential for an act to be 'miraculous'. A verse from the First Epistle of Corinthians seems to agree with Endo on this point:

> If I speak in the tongues of men or of angels, but do not have love, I am only a resounding gong or a clanging cymbal. If I have the gift of prophecy and can fathom all mysteries and all knowledge, and if I have a faith that can move mountains, but do not have love, I am nothing.

What does our observation of extremely altruistic acts show about the definition of a miracle as a violation of the laws of nature, caused by an intentional agent, and possessing religious significance? It does not show that the definition should be rejected altogether because the definition does not entail that miracles are the only religiously significant acts. We can affirm that extremely altruistic acts are as close to miracles as any acts one can perform within the laws of nature, and belief in such acts does not face Hume's argument. This affirmation does not require us to give up our definition of a miracle.

Is altruism a product of evolution?

We have assumed that extremely altruistic acts violate a strong behavioural trait that has been developed through evolution. Critics might reject this assumption, however, by claiming that altruistic acts are themselves merely products of evolution.

In biology, an organism's behaviours are considered altruistic when they increase other organisms' fitness at a cost to the altruistic organism itself. Fitness is measured by the extent to which an organism can produce offspring in a given environment. For example, certain squirrels emit alarm calls to their mates when predators are nearby. This is considered an altruistic act. By emitting alarm calls the altruistic squirrels might save their mates and increase their chance of surviving and reproducing. However, this behaviour may result in reducing their own chance because alarm calls can attract the predators to those emitting the alarm calls. The existence of altruism in nature is puzzling because it seems difficult to explain how altruism, which decreases altruists' own fitness, can remain in nature without contradicting natural selection. Behavioural traits that do not have reproductive advantages do not seem to be able to survive natural selection. Evolutionary biologists have tackled this puzzle by proposing such theories as group selection theory, kin selection theory, and reciprocation theory.

According to group selection theory, natural selection can occur at the level of a group rather than individuals. If a certain individual acts altruistically, then while it might reduce the fitness of the altruistic individual itself it might increase the overall fitness of the group. For example, altruistic wolves bring meat to other members of the pack, and altruistic vampire bats share blood with their sick mates. Behaving altruistically in these ways might reduce the fitness of the altruistic individuals themselves but it might increase the overall fitness of the pack of wolves or group of bats on the whole.

Darwin himself supported group selection theory but its validity has been questioned. If there are altruistic individuals in a group they are likely to be quickly out-produced by others because 'selfish' individuals, which exploit altruistic individuals, would reproduce more successfully than altruistic ones. It is then unclear how altruism can remain in nature.

Kin selection theory is an alternative to group selection theory. This theory was popularized by the British biologist W. D. Hamilton in the 1960s. The following table summarizes the average percentage of genes an individual shares with its kin:

Identical twin: 100%
Parent / child / full sibling: 50%
Grandparent / grandchild / half sibling / aunt / uncle / niece / nephew: 25%
First cousin: 12.5%

These data suggest that, somewhat counterintuitively, from an evolutionary and genetic point of view, sharing resources (such as food) with one's own full sibling, for example, can be as advantageous as sharing them with one's own child. To take another example, sharing resources with one's own grandchild can be more advantageous than sharing them with one's own first cousin but less advantageous than sharing them with one's own full sibling. Since kin are genetically related, genes determining altruism can spread in a family over generations—not unlike how genes determining eye colour can spread in a family over generations. In this way, according to kin selection theory, altruistic behaviours can remain in nature despite their apparent disadvantage to the fitness of altruistic individuals.

Arguably, observing human behaviour provides indirect evidence for kin selection theory. Studies in psychology find that people tend to trust others more easily if they have faces similar to their own or names suggesting the same ethnic backgrounds as their own. Yet kin selection theory is limited as it does not explain altruism among unrelated organisms in the same species or among organisms in distinct species.

Reciprocation theory, which emerged in the 1970s, tries to explain why altruism exists among unrelated organisms and among organisms in distinct species. The theory appeals to a mutually beneficial relationship in the spirit of 'I scratch your back and you scratch mine'. According to this theory, an individual helps another individual if it is probabilistically likely that the favour will be returned at some later time. So called *cleaning symbiosis* represents an altruistic act based on a reciprocatory interaction. For example, small 'cleaner fish' clean 'host fish' by eating parasites located on their mouths and gills. This is mutually beneficial because the host fish gets cleaned and the cleaner fish get fed. The host fish displays altruistic behaviour in this relationship. It does not eat the cleaner fish even though it could, and sometimes it may even save the cleaner fish from predators. Reciprocation theory suggests that the altruistic behaviour of the big fish can be attributed to the mutual benefits it enjoys with the smaller fish.

A crucial question for us here is whether these theories can explain extremely altruistic acts, such as Kolbe's and Williams's. If they can, it is a mistake to think that their acts violate a strong behavioural trait developed through evolution.

Group selection theory says that an individual might perform an altruistic act when it will increase the overall fitness of the group to which the individual belongs. However, again, the theory has been questioned because it fails to explain how altruism can remain despite its disadvantage for the fitness of altruistic individuals. Kin selection theory and reciprocation theory are more widely accepted than group selection theory. Kin selection theory cannot, however, explain extremely altruistic acts because it is limited to altruistic acts between kin. Extremely altruistic acts, such as Kolbe's and Williams's, are altruistic acts directed specifically towards strangers. Reciprocation theory cannot explain extremely altruistic acts either because there is no reciprocatory relationship between extreme altruists and their beneficiaries. Extremely altruistic acts are one-off events in which an altruist dies as a consequence of saving a stranger. Hence, altruistic acts do seem to violate a strong behavioural trait formed through natural selection.

The American scientist George R. Price made significant contributions to the development of kin selection theory. He was, however, seriously troubled by the thought that the theory might entail that altruism is merely a product of natural selection. To eliminate this thought from his mind, he decided to live altruistically. His life ended tragically but it illustrates how humans can act contrary to behavioural traits entailed by evolution.

George R. Price was born in Scarsdale, New York in 1922. After earning a PhD in chemistry at the University of Chicago in his mid-20s he became a physical chemist. He was known as an uncompromising atheist and sceptic. In 1955 and 1956 he published two articles in the journal *Science* criticizing beliefs in psychic phenomena, such as telepathy, clairvoyance, and psychokinesis. In one of the papers, he appealed to Hume's argument against miracles and concluded, 'I hope that my fellow-scientists will similarly withhold belief [in the supernatural]'. Around this time he divorced his wife Julia, who was a practising Roman Catholic. Disagreement over religious belief was one of the factors in their divorce.

Price had an operation for thyroid cancer in 1966 but it was botched. With a large insurance settlement in hand, he relocated to London to start a new life. He had no training in population genetics but he was fascinated by W. D. Hamilton's work on kin selection, which he encountered in a library by accident. He then taught himself the subject and composed what is now known as the 'Price equation'. The Price equation is a mathematical statement describing how the average value of any trait changes over generations in a population of organisms. He reasoned that altruism could be merely an outcome of organisms' adaptations to propagate their genes effectively. Even worse, it seemed to him that 'negative altruism', in which certain organisms sacrifice their own fitness so that other organisms cannot propagate their genes effectively, could occur. Price was deeply bothered by these ideas and decided to 'contradict' them by dedicating his life to helping people in need.

In 1970, Price had a religious experience. He ran through the streets of Marylebone in London looking for a church. He entered the first church that he found and prayed for guidance. He then became a devout Christian. Hamilton, who had become Price's colleague, recalls, 'Always an extremely clear thinker he [Price] was also very explicit, never a man to compromise or to pretend to opinions he didn't hold. This certainly applied to both his anti-religious and his religious periods.' Price believed that everyone who claims to be Christian should follow the teaching of the New Testament literally and concluded that he should live altruistically. He gave money to the homeless and alcoholics, invited them to his flat, and tried to find them jobs. His community work, however, did not go well. Those who came to his flat stole or smashed up his belongings. Price eventually ran out of money and lost his home. He nevertheless told Hamilton that his discovery in population genetics had been God-given because it would otherwise have been impossible for someone like him, who had no formal training in statistics, to discover something that had been overlooked by specialists around the world.

Price tried to hide himself from the alcoholics he had rescued, but his work and private life were constantly disrupted.

In 1975, Price killed himself in a squat in Euston, London, with a pair of nail scissors. His brief suicide note said that he was depressed by the difficulties in his life, particularly those related to community work, and that he felt he was becoming a burden to his friends. His funeral was attended by only a handful of people.

Despite this tragic end, Price seems to have proven through his altruistic acts towards strangers that humans do have the capacity to act contrary to the strong behavioural traits entailed by natural selection. It seems that at least some altruistic acts are not mere outcomes of organisms' adaptations to propagate their genes effectively.

Suppose, for the sake of argument, however, that someone devises a new, more comprehensive evolutionary explanation of altruistic acts. Would such a theory explain away extremely altruistic acts? The answer is 'no' because it would only raise another difficult question: Why are extremely altruistic acts so rare? If it is genetically advantageous for individuals to act extremely altruistically these acts should be observed regularly. Yet, extremely altruistic acts are only rarely observed. Also, any evolutionary account of altruism is likely to entail that acting altruistically to a certain level can be genetically advantageous. It is unlikely, however, that any plausible theory entails that acting altruistically to an extreme level can be genetically advantageous. As Kolbe's and Williams's examples show, a human has the capacity, by an act of will power, to behave altruistically to an extreme level. Hence, again, it seems impossible to explain away extremely altruistic acts by appealing to evolution.

In his memoir *Man's Search for Meaning*, the Holocaust survivor Viktor Frankl writes:

> We who lived in concentration camps can remember the men who walked through the huts comforting others, giving away their last

piece of bread. They may have been few in number, but they offer
sufficient proof that everything can be taken from a man but one
thing: the last of the human freedoms—to choose one's attitude in
any given set of circumstances, to choose one's own way.

Behavioural traits formed through evolution compel humans to
act in a certain way but they still retain free will to defy them.
As Frankl says, humans have the capacity to choose to act freely
and altruistically even in the most life-threatening situations.
Such acts cannot be deemed miracles on our definition but
performing an altruistic act remains the closest one can come
to performing a miracle without violating the laws of nature.

Is altruism an incoherent concept?

We have seen that scientists have proposed theories showing
that certain altruistic acts are products of natural selection.
As we have seen, however, they fail to show that extremely altruistic
acts, such as Kolbe's and Williams's, are also products of natural
selection. At this point, critics might try to advance the following
conceptual, as opposed to scientific, criticism: There can never be
an act that is genuinely altruistic because the concept of altruism
is self-contradictory. Extremely altruistic acts impress us because
it seems that in these acts altruists benefit strangers in the most
significant way (saving their lives) while paying the most significant
cost themselves (sacrificing their own lives). According to the
criticism in question, however, any acts that humans perform,
including even extremely altruistic acts, are motivated by
self-interest or egocentric desires. For example, the criticism
continues, Kolbe's and Williams's extremely altruistic acts saved
others because they desired to save them and they wanted to fulfil
that desire—even if that meant sacrificing their own lives. Otherwise,
they would not have acted in the way they did. Indeed, Kolbe is
reported to have said, 'I *want* to go instead of the man who was
selected [to be sent to the starvation bunker]' (emphasis added).
Therefore, the criticism concludes, the concept of altruism, which

is understood not to be motivated by self-interest or egocentric desires, is self-contradictory.

While there is something correct about this criticism there is also something incorrect about it. It is correct to say that Kolbe and Williams wanted to save the people they saved and that they did wish to fulfil their own desires: they did 'want' to save them. What is incorrect with the criticism, however, is that it presupposes that wishing to fulfil a desire is always entirely egocentric. Kolbe and Williams 'wanted' to save the victims but 'want' here is not the same as the ordinary sense of 'want' which is linked to the pleasure that one enjoys when fulfilling one's desire. It is reasonable to assume that Kolbe and Williams 'wanted' to save the victims not in the sense that saving them would give them pleasure but in the sense that they thought that they could save the lives of victims who ought not to die.

Of course, it is in principle possible that Kolbe and Williams had hidden egocentric motivations behind their altruistic acts. For example, perhaps Kolbe wanted to sacrifice his life so that he would be blessed by God in heaven. Or perhaps Williams wanted to sacrifice his life so that he could die a hero. Even so, their acts evoke deep awe because, given that they had to sacrifice their very lives, it is unlikely that their egocentric concerns were the *sole* motivations for their extremely altruistic acts. The concept of altruism is self-contradictory if all possible altruistic acts are motivated solely by self-interest or egocentric desires but that is highly implausible given the sacrifice that altruists have to make, particularly in extreme situations like Kolbe's and Williams's.

Critics might pursue another strategy to 'explain away' Kolbe's and Williams's extreme altruism. One might argue, for example, that Kolbe sacrificed his life because, on his calculation, Gajowniczek, the prisoner whom he saved, was worth more than himself; Gajowniczek had a family and was therefore indispensable to other people, whereas he had no one.

This might well be the case but it does not undermine the claim that Kolbe's act defied the strong behavioural trait that humans have developed through a long process of evolution. To take another example, one might argue that Williams miscalculated his ability to survive. His bravery and possible bravado spurred him on to help others before himself and eventually led to his own death. However, even if Williams's act was based on a miscalculation, given the observation of the difficult rescue process in the severe weather, he must have been aware that he was risking his own life by saving others. What he did, therefore, remains an extremely altruistic act.

Miracles, altruism, and the golden rule in the world's great religions

Nature is a cruel place where organisms compete for survival. Given limited resources they are motivated to act egocentrically. They have to prioritize self-interest so that they can win the survival game. The leaders of the world's great religions, however, teach us to act in the opposite direction. They teach us to avoid egoism and follow the so-called *Golden Rule*: treat others as you would wish them to treat you. This rule is sometimes presented in a negative form: do *not* treat others as you would *not* wish them to treat you. Both positive and negative forms of the Golden Rule are found in the teachings of virtually all the world's great religions.

In Judaism, the book of Leviticus reports that God commanded Moses to tell the Israelites, 'Do not seek revenge or bear a grudge against anyone among your people, but love your neighbour as yourself'. God is also reported to have told them, 'The foreigner residing among you must be treated as your native-born. Love them as yourself, for you were foreigners in Egypt.' The Babylonian Talmud reports that the Jewish sage Hillel the Elder presented a negative form of the Golden Rule. A man told Hillel that he would convert to Judaism if Hillel could teach him the entire Torah while he was standing on one foot. Hillel then said,

'That which is hateful to you, do not do to your fellow. That is the whole Torah; the rest is the explanation; go and learn it.'

In Christianity, the Gospel of Matthew reports that Jesus presented the Golden Rule in his Sermon on the Mount: 'So in everything, do to others what you would have them do to you, for this sums up the Law and the Prophets'. Jesus is also reported to have said, 'Do to others as you would have them do to you'. The Gospel of Luke also introduces Jesus's parable of the Good Samaritan, which illustrates the Golden Rule. A man was attacked by robbers while travelling from Jerusalem to Jericho. He was stripped, beaten, and left half dead. People saw the man but they passed on by. A Samaritan, who took pity on him, however, treated the man's wound, put him on his own donkey, and took him to an inn to take care of him. He gave coins to the innkeeper asking him to look after the man and telling him that he would reimburse any extra expense later. Jesus taught people to act like this Samaritan.

In Islam, the Quran reads, 'Worship God, and ascribe no partners to Him, and be good to the parents, and the relatives, and the orphans, and the poor, and the neighbour next door, and the distant neighbour, and the close associate, and the traveller, and your servants. God does not love the arrogant showoff.' Muhammad is reported to have said in hadith, 'None of you has faith until he loves for his brother what he loves for himself' and 'Whoever wishes to be delivered from the fire and enter the garden should die with faith in Allah and the Last Day and should treat the people as he wishes to be treated by them'.

The Golden Rule is found in Eastern religions as well. For example, the Buddha is reported to have said, 'One should seek for others the happiness one desires for oneself'. We can also find the rule presented in negative terms in Buddhist texts. For example, the *Udānavarga* reads, 'Hurt not others in ways that you yourself would find hurtful'. Similarly, the *Sutta Nipata* reads, 'Comparing oneself to others in such terms as "Just as I am so are they, just as they are so am I", he should neither kill nor cause others to kill'.

In Hinduism, the Golden Rule is found in several books of the *Mahābhārata*, a Sanskrit epic poem of ancient India. The Rule is consistently presented in a negative form: 'One should not direct towards someone else what is unpleasant to oneself: this would be, in summary, the moral duty; the other proceeds from desire'; 'One should himself not do what he would disapprove of in others; for he incurs ridicule if he expresses criticism in this condition'.

Altruistic acts can be construed as exemplifications of the Golden Rule. People ordinarily act for their own well-being. Altruists, who consciously or unconsciously follow the Golden Rule, however, act for others' well-being. Extremely altruistic acts such as Kolbe's and Williams's are the most radical forms of selflessness in which altruists sacrifice their own lives for the well-being of strangers.

The leaders of the world's great religions do not wish to deny the possibility of miracles and many believe that such leaders indeed perform miracles themselves if necessary. When it comes to what humans can do, however, they encourage us to focus less on miracles and more on performing altruistic acts, which do not have to violate the laws of nature. As the Kolbe and Williams examples show, that they performed their acts within the laws of nature does not undermine their significance. Those who benefited from them experienced them *as* miracles, and when we read about them they seem 'miraculous' enough to inspire awe.

All the well-known examples of miracles violate the laws of nature. Yet acts that do not violate the laws of nature can be equally, or possibly even more, awe-inspiring—even though they cannot be called miracles in a strict sense. These acts are, moreover, not vulnerable to Hume's argument against belief in miracles precisely because they take place within the laws of nature. Therefore, perhaps, somewhat contradictorily, what we may consider truly 'miraculous' and what we can believe in rationally are acts that do not require the supernatural. As Kolbe and Williams have shown, such acts can in principle be performed by ordinary people like us.

References and further reading

Preface

For scholars' remarks on miracles in modern society, see:

Bultmann, Rudolf (1941/1953), 'New Testament and Mythology', *Kerygma and Myth: A Theological Debate*, ed. Hans Werner Bartsch and trans. Reginald H. Fuller (New York: Harper & Row), 1–44.

Dawkins, Richard (2006), *The God Delusion* (New York: Bantam Books).

For statistics on the prevalence of belief in miracles, see:

Harris Poll (2013), 'Americans' Belief in God, Miracles and Heaven Declines', <http://www.theharrispoll.com/health-and-life/ Americans__Belief_in_God__Miracles_and_Heaven_Declines. html>.

Pew Forum on Religion and Public Life (2008), 'U.S. Religious Landscape Survey: Religious Beliefs and Practices: Diverse and Politically Relevant', <http://www.pewforum.org/files/2008/06/ report2-religious-landscape-study-full.pdf>.

Theos (2013), 'The Spirit of Things Unseen: Belief in Post-Religious Britain', <http://www.theosthinktank.co.uk/files/files/Reports/ Spirit%20of%20Things%20-%20Digital%20(update).pdf>.

Chapter 1: What are miracles?

For reports of unusual events that are described as miracles, see:

BBC News (2004), '"Virgin Mary" Toast Fetches $28,000', 22 November, <http://news.bbc.co.uk/1/hi/4034787.stm>.

Crompton, Jenny (2013), *Unbelievable: The Bizarre World of Coincidences* (London: Michael O'Mara Books).

Greene, Bob (1978), 'They Come to Worship at the Tortilla Shrine', *Free Lance-Star* 17 July.

Holland, R. F. (1965), 'The Miraculous', *American Philosophical Quarterly* 2: 43–51.

Mitchell, John and Robert J. M. Rickard (1977), *Phenomena: A Book of Wonders* (New York: Pantheon Books).

Mora, Camilo, Derek P. Tittensor, Sina Adl, Alastair G. B. Simpson, and Boris Worm (2011), 'How Many Species are there on Earth and in the Oscean?', *PLOS Biology* 9: 1–8.

Nichols, Luke (2010), 'Remember the Miracle: Church Explosion 60 Years Ago not Forgotten', *Beatrice Daily Sun*, 1 March.

Plimmer, Martin and Brian King (2004), *Beyond Coincidence* (Cambridge: Icon Books).

Reader's Digest (1982), *Mysteries of the Unexplained: How Ordinary Men and Women Have Experienced the Strange, the Uncanny, and the Incredible* (Pleasantville, NY: The Reader's Digest Association).

For Aquinas's view on what God can and cannot do, see:

Aquinas, Thomas (13th century/1975), *Summa Contra Gentiles*, trans. James F. Anderson (Notre Dame, IN: University of Notre Dame Press), quoted passage on p. 8 ('[God] cannot make one and the same thing to be and not to be…').

Mavrodes, George I. (1963), 'Some Puzzles Concerning Omnipotence', *Philosophical Review* 72: 221–3.

For Hume's definition of a miracle, see:

Hume, David (1748/2012), *An Enquiry Concerning Human Understanding* (Cambridge: Cambridge University Press), quoted passage on p. 101 ('A miracle may be accurately defined…').

Chapter 2: What miracles are reported in religious texts?

For miracle reports in the world's great religions, see:

Al-Yahsubi, Qadi Iyad Ibn Musa (1991), *Muhammad: Messenger of Allah (Ash-Shifa of Qadi Iyad)*, trans. Aisha Bewley (Granada: Madinah Press).

Ashe, Geoffrey (1978), *Miracles* (London: Routledge and Kegan Paul).

BBC News (2015), 'Pope Francis Recognises Second Mother Teresa "Miracle"', 18 December, <http://www.bbc.co.uk/news/world-asia-india-35129463>.

Chinese Buddhist Encyclopedia, <http://www.chinabuddhismencyclopedia.com/>.

Dallmayr, Fred (2007), *In Search of the Good Life: A Pedagogy for Troubled Times* (Lexington, KY: University of Kentucky Press).

Geivett, R. Douglas and Gary R. Habermas (eds) (1997), *In Defense of Miracles: A Comprehensive Case for God's Action in History* (Downers Grove, IL: InterVarsity Press).

Grosso, Michael (2015), *The Man Who Could Fly: St. Joseph of Copertino and the Mystery of Levitation* (Lanham, MD: Rowman and Littlefield).

Hayes, Patrick J. (2016), *Miracles: An Encyclopedia of People, Places, and Supernatural Events from Antiquity to the Present* (Santa Barbara, CA: ABC-CLIO).

Hess, Linda Singh (2002), *The Bijak of Kabir* (Oxford: Oxford University Press).

Keener, Craig S. (2011), *Miracles: The Credibility of the New Testament Accounts*, Volumes 1 and 2 (Grand Rapids, MI: Baker Academic).

Leach, Edmund (1966), 'Virgin Birth', *Proceedings of the Royal Anthropological Institute of Great Britain and Ireland for 1966* (London: Royal Anthropological Institute of Great Britain and Ireland), pp. 39–49.

Lowis, Michael J. (2014), *The Gospel Miracles: What Really Happened? A Systematic, Open-Minded Review of the Evidence* (Eugene, OR: Resource Publications).

Macdonald, Dennis R. (2015), *Mythologizing Jesus: From Jewish Teacher to Epic Hero* (Lanham, MD: Rowman and Littlefield).

Nickell, Joe (1998), *Looking for Miracles: Weeping Icons, Relics, Stigmata, Visions and Healing Cures* (Amherst, NY: Prometheus Books).

Nickell, Joe (2013), *The Science of Miracles: Investigating the Incredible* (Amherst, NY: Prometheus Books).

Nursi, Said (2001), *The Letters 1928–1932*, trans. Şükran Vahide (Istanbul: Sözler Publications).

O'Neill, Michael (2015), *Exploring the Miraculous* (Huntington, IN: Our Sunday Visitor Publishing Division).

Poythress, Vern S. (2016), *The Miracle of Jesus: How the Savior's Mighty Acts Serve as Signs of Redemption* (Wheaton, IL: Crossway).

Schimmel, Annemarie (1975), *Mystical Dimensions of Islam* (Chapel Hill, NC: University of North Carolina Press).

Telegraph (2009), 'Koran Verses "Appear" on Skin of Miracle Russian Baby', 22 October.

Treece, Patricia (1988), *Nothing Short of a Miracle: God's Healing Power in Modern Saints* (Manchester, NH: Sophia Institute Press).

Twelftree, Graham H. (ed.) (2011), *The Cambridge Companion to Miracles* (Cambridge: Cambridge University Press).

Warrington, Keith (2015), *The Miracles in the Gospels: What do they Teach us About Jesus?* (London: Society for Promoting Christian Knowledge).

Weddle, David L. (2010), *Miracles: Wonder and Meaning in World Religions* (New York: New York University Press).

Woodward, Kenneth L. (2000), *The Book of Miracles: The Meaning of the Miracle Stories in Christianity, Judaism, Buddhism, Hinduism and Islam* (New York: Touchstone).

Chapter 3: Why do so many people believe in miracles?

For psychological studies on infants' detection of violations of the laws of nature, see:

Baillargeon, Renée (2004), '"Infants" Reasoning about Hidden Objects: Evidence for Event-General and Event-Specific Expectations', *Developmental Sciences* 7: 391–424.

Hespos, Susan J. and Renée Baillargeon (2001), 'Reasoning about Containment Events in Very Young Infants', *Cognition* 78: 207–45.

Stahl, Aimee E. and Lisa Feigenson (2015), 'Observing the Unexpected Enhances Infants' Learning and Exploration', *Science* 348: 91–4.

Wang, Su-hua, Renée Baillargeon, and Sarah Paterson (2005), 'Detecting Continuity Violations in Infancy: A New Account and New Evidence from Covering and Tube Events', *Cognition* 95: 129–73.

Wilcox, Teresa, Lynn Nadel, and Rosemary Rosser (1996), 'Location Memory in Healthy Preterm and Full-Term Infants', *Infant Behavior and Development* 19: 309–23.

For the minimal counterintuitiveness theory, see:

Barrett, Justin L. and Melanie A. Nyhof (2001), 'Spreading Non-Natural Concepts: The Role of Intuitive Conceptual Structures in Memory and Transmission of Cultural Materials', *Journal of Cognition and Culture* 1: 69–100.

Boyer, Pascal (1994), *The Naturalness of Religious Ideas: A Cognitive Theory of Religion* (Berkeley, CA: University of California Press).

Boyer, Pascal and Charles Ramble (2010), 'Cognitive Templates for Religious Concepts: Cross-Cultural Evidence for Recall of Counter-Intuitive Representations', *Cognitive Science* 25: 535–64.

Lisdorf, Anders (2004), 'The Spreads of Non-Natural Concepts: Evidence from the Roman Prodigy Lists', *Journal of Cognition and Culture* 4: 151–74.

Pyysiäinen, Ilkka (2004), *Magic, Miracles, and Religion: A Scientific Perspective* (Lanham, MD: AltaMira Press).

For the hyperactive agency detection device and pareidolia, see:

Barrett, Justin L. (2004), *Why Would Anyone Believe in God?* (Lanham, MD: AltaMira Press).

Barrett, Justin L. (2007), 'Cognitive Science of Religion: What is it and Why is it?', *Religion Compass* 1: 768–86.

Bering, Jesse (2011), *The Belief Instinct: The Psychology of Souls, Destiny, and the Meaning of Life* (New York: W. W. Norton and Company).

Clark, Ronald W. (1977), *Edison: The Man Who Made the Future* (New York: G. P. Putnam's Sons).

Guthrie, S. E. (1993), *Faces in the Clouds: A New Theory of Religion* (New York: Oxford University Press).

Lescarboura, Austin C. (1920), 'Edison's Views on Life and Death', *Scientific American* 30 October, 123, quoted passage on p. 446 ('I have been thinking for some time...').

For the cognitive bias towards detecting intention and purpose in nature, see:

Kelemen, Deborah (1999), 'Why Are Rocks Pointy? Children's Preference for Teleological Explanations of the Natural World', *Developmental Psychology* 35: 1440–53.

Kelemen, Deborah (2003), 'British and American Children's Preferences for Teleo-Functional Explanations of the Natural World', *Cognition* 88: 201–21.

Kelemen, Deborah (2004), 'Are Children "Intuitive Theists"? Reasoning About Purpose and Design in Nature', *Psychological Science* 15: 295–301.

Kelemen, Deborah and Evelyn Rosset (2009), 'The Human Function Compunction: Teleological Explanation in Adults', *Cognition* 111: 138–43.

Paget, Jean (1929), *The Child's Conception of the World* (New York: Harcourt Brace).

Chapter 4: Is it rational to believe in miracles?

For the life and work of Hume, see:

Ayer, A. J. (2000, originally 1980), *Hume: A Very Short Introduction* (Oxford: Oxford University Press).

Boswell, James (1994), *The Journals of James Boswell: 1762–1795* (New Haven, CN: Yale University Press).

Earman, John (2000), *Hume's Abject Failure: The Argument Against Miracles* (Oxford: Oxford University Press).

Fogelin, Robert J. (2003), *A Defense of Hume on Miracles* (Princeton, NJ: Princeton University Press).

Harris, James A. (2015), *Hume: An Intellectual Biography* (Cambridge: Cambridge University Press).

Houston, J. (1994), *Reported Miracles: A Critique of Hume* (Cambridge: Cambridge University Press).

Hume, David (1748/2012), *An Enquiry Concerning Human Understanding* (Cambridge: Cambridge University Press).

Mossner, Ernest Campbell (1954/2001), *The Life of David Hume*, Second Edition (Oxford: Oxford University Press).

Taylor, James E. (2007), 'Hume on Miracles: Interpretation and Criticism', *Philosophy Compass* 2: 611–24.

For Carl Sagan's scepticism about the supernatural, see:

Sagan, Carl (1996), *The Demon-Haunted World: Science as a Candle in the Dark* (New York: Ballantine Books).

Sagan, Carl (2006), *The Varieties of Scientific Experience: A Personal View of the Search for God* (New York: Penguin Books).

Head, Tom (ed.) (2006), *Conversations with Carl Sagan* (Jackson, MS: University of Mississippi Press), quoted passage on p. 47 ('There's not a smidgen of evidence to suggest...').

For philosophical debates on miracles, see:

Basinger, David and Randall Basinger (1986), *Philosophy and Miracle: The Contemporary Debate* (New York: Edwin Mellen Press).

Brown, Colin (1984), *Miracles and the Critical Mind* (Grand Rapids, MI: Wm. B. Eerdmans).

Corder, David (2007), *The Philosophy of Miracles* (London: Continuum).

Geivett, R. Douglas and Gary R. Habermas (1997), *In Defense of Miracles: A Comprehensive Case for God's Action in History* (Downer Grove, IL: InterVarsity Press).

Larmer, Robert A. (1988), *Water into Wine? An Investigation of the Concept of Miracle* (Kingston, ON: McGill-Queen's University Press).

Lewis, C. S. (1998, originally 1947), *Miracles* (London: Fount).

Luck, Morgan (2011), 'Defining Miracles: Violations of the Laws of Nature', *Philosophy Compass* 6: 133–41.

Luck, Morgan (2016), 'Defining Miracles: Direct vs. Indirect Causation', *Philosophy Compass* 11: 267–76.

McGrew, Timothy (2015), 'Miracles', *The Stanford Encyclopedia of Philosophy*, Winter Edition, ed. Edward N. Zalta, <http://plato.stanford.edu/archives/win2015/entries/miracles/>.

Swinburne, Richard (1970), *The Concept of Miracles* (London: Macmillan).

Swinburne, Richard (ed.) (1989), *Miracles* (New York: Macmillan).

Chapter 5: Can there be miracles without the supernatural?

For the life and work of Maximilian Kolbe, see:

Binder, David (1995), 'Franciszek Gajowniczek Dead; Priest Died for Him at Auschwitz', *New York Times*, 15 March, <http://www.nytimes.com/1995/03/15/obituaries/franciszek-gajowniczek-dead-priest-died-for-him-at-auschwitz.html>.

Chenu, Bruno, Claude Prud'homme, France Quéré, and Jean-Claude Thomas (1990), *The Book of Christian Martyrs*, trans. John Bowden (London: SMC Press), quoted passage on p. 170 ('The ten condemned to death went through terrible days…').

Craig, Mary (ed.) (1997), '"Maximilian Kolbe" in Catholic Truth Society', *Maximilian Kolbe, Franz Jägerstätter, Karl Leisner and Rupert Mayer* (London: Catholic Truth Society), pp. 5–21.

Endo, Shusaku (1983), *Watashi Ni Totte Kami Towa* (*What is God for Me*) (Tokyo: Kobunsha), quoted passage on p. 75 ('I can never perform an act like Kolbe's…').

Endo, Shusaku (1976), *Watashi No Iesu: Nihonjin No Tame No Seisho Nyumon* (*Jesus for Me: An Introduction to the Bible for the Japanese*) (Tokyo: Shodensha), quoted passage on p. 166 ('I would not think of it as a miracle…').

Stone, Elaine Murray (1997), *Maximilian Kolbe: Saint of Auschwitz* (New York: Paulist Press).

For Viktor Frankl's life in an Auschwitz concentration camp, see:

Frankl, Viktor (1946/1984), *Man's Search for Meaning: An Introduction for Logotherapy* (New York: Pocket Books), quoted passage on p. 86 ('We who lived in concentration camps can remember the men...').

For scientific studies of altruism, see:

Boehm, Christopher (2012), *Moral Origins: The Evolution of Virtue, Altruism, and Shame* (New York: Basic Books).

Bowles, Samuel and Gintis, Herbert (2011), *A Cooperative Species: Human Reciprocity and its Evolution* (Princeton, NJ: Princeton University Press).

Dugatkin, Lee Alan (2006), *The Altruism Equation: Seven Scientists Search for the Origins of Goodness* (Princeton, NJ: Princeton University Press).

Farrelly, Daniel, Paul Clemson, and Melissa Guthrie (2016), 'Are Women's Mate Preferences for Altruism Also Influenced by Physical Attractiveness?', *Evolutionary Psychology* 77: 1–6.

Okasha, Samir (2013), 'Biological Altruism', *The Stanford Encyclopedia of Philosophy*, Fall Edition, ed. Edward N. Zalta, <http://plato.stanford.edu/archives/fall2013/entries/altruism-biological/>.

Pfaff, Donald W. (2015), *The Altruistic Brain: How We Are Naturally Good* (Oxford: Oxford University Press).

Post, Stephn G., Lynn G. Underwood, Jeffrey P. Schloss, and William B. Hurlbut (2002), *Altruism and Altruistic Love: Science, Philosophy, and Religion in Dialogue* (New York: Oxford University Press).

Vakoch, Douglas A. (ed.) (2013), *Altruism in Cross-Cultural Perspective* (New York: Springer).

Wilson, Davis Sloan (2015), *Does Altruism Exist? Culture, Genes, and the Welfare of Others* (New Haven, CT: Yale University Press).

For the theory of evolution, see:

Darwin, Charles (1859/2009), *The Origin of Species* (Oxford: Oxford University Press).

Dawkins, Richard (1976), *The Selfish Gene* (Oxford: Oxford University Press).

Futuyma, Douglas J. (2013), *Evolution*, Third Edition (Sunderland, MA: Sinauer Associates).

Miele, Frank (1995), 'Darwin's Dangerous Disciple: An Interview with Richard Dawkins', *Scepsis*, <https://scepsis.net/eng/articles/id_3.php/>.

For the life and work of George R. Price, see:

Brown, Andrew (1999), *The Darwin Wars: The Scientific Battle for the Soul of Man* (London: Simon and Schuster).

Hamilton, William Donald (1996), *Narrow Roads of Gene Land*, Volume 1: *Evolution of Social Behaviour* (Oxford: W. H. Freeman and Company).

Harman, Oren (2010), *The Price of Altruism: Geroge Price and the Search for the Origins of Kindness* (London: Vintage).

Markowitz, Miriam (2010), 'The Group: On George Price', *The Nation*, 22 September, <https://www.thenation.com/article/group-george-price/>.

For philosophical debates on altruism, see:

Blum, Lawrence (1980/2009), *Friendship, Altruism and Morality* (London: Routledge).

Kraut, Richard (2016), 'Altruism', *The Stanford Encyclopedia of Philosophy*, Fall Edition, ed. Edward N. Zalta, <http://plato.stanford.edu/archives/fall2016/entries/altruism/>.

Maibom, Heidi (ed.) (2017), *The Routledge Handbook of Philosophy of Empathy* (London: Routledge).

Nagel, Thomas (1970), *The Possibility of Altruism* (Oxford: Oxford University Press).

Oord, Thomas (ed.) (2008), *The Altruism Reader: Selections from Writings on Love, Religion, and Science* (West Conshohocken, PA: Templeton Press).

For the Golden Rule in the world's great religions, see:

Bakker, Freek L. (2013), 'Comparing the Golden Rule in Hindu and Christian Religious Texts', *Studies in Religion* 42: 38–58.

Gensler, Harry J. (2013), *Ethics and the Golden Rule* (London: Routledge).

Neusner, Jacob and Bruce Chilton (eds) (2005), *Altruism in World Religions* (Washington, DC: Georgetown University Press).

Neusner, Jacob and Bruce Chilton (2008), *The Golden Rule: The Ethics of Reciprocity in World Religions* (London: Continuum).

Wattles, Jeffrey (1996), *The Golden Rule* (Oxford: Oxford University Press).

Miracles

Index

Index

Agnosticism
A Very Short Introduction
Robin Le Poidevin

What is agnosticism? Is it just the 'don't know' position on God, or is there more to it than this? Is it a belief, or merely the absence of belief? Who were the first to call themselves 'agnostics'? These are just some of the questions that Robin Le Poidevin considers in this *Very Short Introduction*. He sets the philosophical case for agnosticism and explores it as a historical and cultural phenomenon. What emerges is a much more sophisticated, and much more interesting, attitude than a simple failure to either commit to, or reject, religious belief. Le Poidevin challenges some preconceptions and assumptions among both believers and non-atheists, and invites the reader to rethink their own position on the issues.

CATHOLICISM
A Very Short Introduction
Gerald O'Collins

Despite a long history of external threats and internal strife, the Roman Catholic Church and the broader reality of Catholicism remain a vast and valuable presence into the third millennium of world history. What are the origins of the Catholic Church? How has Catholicism changed and adapted to such vast and diverse cultural influences over the centuries? What great challenges does the Catholic Church now face in the twenty-first century, both within its own life and in its relation to others around the world? In this Very Short Introduction, Gerald O'Collins draws on the best current scholarship available to answer these questions and to present, in clear and accessible language, a fresh introduction to the largest and oldest institution in the world.

CHRISTIAN ETHICS
A Very Short Introduction
D. Stephen Long

This *Very Short Introduction* to Christian ethics introduces the topic by examining its sources and historical basis. D. Stephen Long presents a discussion of the relationship between Christian ethics, modern, and postmodern ethics, and explores practical issues including sex, money, and power. Long recognises the inherent difficulties in bringing together 'Christian' and 'ethics' but argues that this is an important task for both the Christian faith and for ethics. Arguing that Christian ethics are not a precise science, but the cultivation of practical wisdom from a range of sources, Long also discusses some of the failures of the Christian tradition, including the crusades, the conquest, slavery, inquisitions, and the Galileo affair.

www.oup.com/vsi

DRUIDS
A Very Short Introduction
Barry Cunliffe

The Druids first came into focus in Western Europe - Gaul, Britain, and Ireland - in the second century BC. They are a popular subject; they have been known and discussed for over 2,000 years and few figures flit so elusively through history. They are enigmatic and puzzling, partly because of the lack of knowledge about them has resulted in a wide spectrum of interpretations. Barry Cunliffe takes the reader through the evidence relating to the Druids, trying to decide what can be said and what can't be said about them. He examines why the nature of the druid caste changed quite dramatically over time, and how successive generations have interpreted the phenomenon in very different ways.

www.oup.com/vsi

CLASSICAL MYTHOLOGY
A Very Short Introduction
Helen Morales

From Zeus and Europa, to Diana, Pan, and Prometheus, the myths of ancient Greece and Rome seem to exert a timeless power over us. But what do those myths represent, and why are they so enduringly fascinating? This imaginative and stimulating *Very Short Introduction* is a wide-ranging account, examining how classical myths are used and understood in both high art and popular culture, taking the reader from the temples of Crete to skyscrapers in New York, and finding classical myths in a variety of unexpected places: from Arabic poetry and Hollywood films, to psychoanalysis, the bible, and New Age spiritualism.

www.oup.com/vsi

KABBALAH
A Very Short Introduction
Joseph Dan

In *Kabbalah*, Joseph Dan debunks the myths surrounding modern Kabbalistic practice, offering an engaging and dependable account of this traditional Jewish religious phenomenon and its impact outside of Judaism. Dan sheds light on the many misconceptions about what Kabbalah is and isn't—including its connections to magic, astronomy, alchemy, and numerology—and he illuminates the relationship between Kabbalah and Christianity on the one hand and New Age religion on the other. Dan examines its fascinating historical background, including key ancient texts of this tradition. He concludes with a brief survey of scholarship in the field and a list of books for further reading.

> "Dan has given us the best concise history of Jewish mysticism. . . . As a 'very short introduction' to this sublime treasure house, Joseph Dan's book is warmly recommended."

> Benjamin Balint, Commentary

FUNDAMENTALISM
A Very Short Introduction
Malise Ruthven

Malise Ruthven tackles the polemic and stereotypes surrounding this complex phenomenon - one that eludes him today, a conclusion impossible to ignore since the events in New York on September 11 2001. But what does 'fundamentalism' really mean? Since it was coined by American Protestant evangelicals in the 1920s, the use of the term 'fundamentalist' has expanded to include a diverse range of radical conservatives and ideological purists, not all religious. Ruthven investigates fundamentalism's historical, social, religious, political, and ideological roots, and tackles the polemic and stereotypes surrounding this complex phenomenon - one that eludes simple definition, yet urgently needs to be understood.

'...powerful stuff...this book is perceptive and important.'

Observer

Expand your collection of
VERY SHORT INTRODUCTIONS